HUMANE CAPITAL

HUMANE CAPITAL

How to Create a Management Shift to Transform Performance and Profit

VLATKA HLUPIC

BLOOMSBURY BUSINESS

LONDON • NEW YORK • OXFORD • NEW DELHI • SYDNEY

BLOOMSBURY BUSINESS
Bloomsbury Publishing Plc
50 Bedford Square, London, WC1B 3DP, UK
1385 Broadway, New York, NY 10018, USA

BLOOMSBURY, BLOOMSBURY BUSINESS and the Diana logo are trademarks of
Bloomsbury Publishing Plc

First published in Great Britain 2019

A catalogue record for this book is available from the British Library.

A catalog record for this book is available from the Library of Congress.

ISBN: HB: 978-1-4729-5764-1
          ePDF: 978-1-4729-5765-8
          eBook: 978-1-4729-5766-5

Typeset by RefineCatch Limited, Bungay, Suffolk
Printed and bound in Great Britain

To find out more about our authors and books visit www.bloomsbury.com
and sign up for our newsletters.

To Humanity

CONTENTS

PRAISE FOR *HUMANE CAPITAL*

'*Humane Capital* is a really thought-provoking analysis of the management challenges facing companies, large and small, in today's fast-moving economy. Most managers recognise the tensions between long and short term thinking, and between people and profits. Vlatka Hlupic provides some valuable advice for how to resolve these tensions, to make companies more sustainable and more humane.'

PROFESSOR JULIAN BIRKINSHAW, *Professor of Strategy and Entrepreneurship and Deputy Dean at the London Business School, Thinkers50 management thought leader*

'A powerful, and provocative, blend of case studies, research, and practical implications for making business more personal and personal more humane.'
DAVID BURKUS, *author of* Friend of A Friend *and* Under New Management

'In an era when corporations increasingly treat employees as just another means to their financial ends, and work becomes both more contingent and precarious and ever more controlled, here is a bracing and timely antidote. Treating people well at work is the right thing to do, says Hlupic, with plentiful case studies in support, and there is no downside. No excuses: just do it.'

SIMON CAULKIN, *senior editor GPDF, former management columnist for* The Observer

'*Humane Capital* presents a well-researched argument for the growing importance of humanizing business and Vlatka's narrative incorporates several compelling case studies that demonstrate that "doing good" is actually "good business".'
SANGEET PAUL CHOUDARY, *best-selling author of* Platform Revolution *and* Platform Scale, *World Economic Forum Young Global Leader, Top 10 HBR contributor, Founder of Platformation Labs*

'The importance of human quality is critical to organizational success. Vlatka's *Humane Capital* will make a difference for business leaders and organizations.'

SUBIR CHOWDHURY, *best-selling author, CEO of ASI Consulting Group, Thinkers50 management thought leader*

'*Humane Capital* is an outstanding read from a management scholar who has worked extensively with leaders and businesses. It highlights the thoughts and reflections of 59 business leaders in a lively and entertaining way, many nuggets of wisdom here!'

PROFESSOR SIR CARY COOPER CBE, *50th Anniversary Professor of Organizational Psychology & Health, ALLIANCE Manchester Business School, President of the CIPD, President of the British Academy of Management, Immediate Past President of RELATE, President of the Institute of Welfare, Lifetime Achievement Award recipient from* HR *Magazine*

'Vlatka's book is a timely reminder of how more so than ever it is imperative that businesses wake up to their broader societal responsibilities and recognise that it is possible to do well by doing good. Social good and impact should not be seen as a nice to have or trade-off and is something companies at all stages can embrace as highlighted by the case studies in the book; shining a light on the best practices within the non-profit, SME and corporate world.'

RAJEEB DEY MBE, *founder & CEO of Learnerbly & World Economic Forum Young Global Leader*

'Vlatka Hlupic's new book is full of interesting insights and observations. The book will be interesting for all who want to be a successful manager in today's rapidly changing world.'

OLEG ELSHIN, *Nobel Prize nominee, President, CEO at Terra Seismic*

'Vlatka's contribution pushes an open door in the direction of how the Fourth Industrial Revolution envisions the role of organizations in the 21st century: Maximizing Human Well-Being. The underlying understanding that building organizations around human centered systems is of cardinal importance, is what makes of this book a wonderful journey, entrenched in some of the most emerging organizational theories as well as applications on the nature of firms today. A must read.'

PROFESSOR MARK ESPOSITO, *Professor of Business and Economics, Harvard University's Division of Continuing Education, an Institutes Council co-leader at the Microeconomics of Competitiveness program at Harvard University*

'How do you humanize an organization where employees are passionate to work? How do you build a high-performance culture that combines profits and principles? Using dozens of engaging case studies, Vlatka addresses these critical questions in this excellent book.'

PROFESSOR SUNIL GUPTA, *the Edward W. Carter Professor of Business Administration and Chair of the General Management Program at Harvard Business School*

'In *Humane Capital*, Vlatka gives us a provocative series of insights from the narratives of leaders within different types of businesses. Building on her transformative work in *The Management Shift*, this is a rich and compelling call-to-action for anyone looking for success in management and fulfilment as a human being.'

PHIL JAMES, *CEO of The Institute of Leadership and Management*

'This is a timely book – engagement levels remain stubbornly low – a crushing waste of human potential. This passionate book seeks to address this problem and to create work places which are life affirming. The argument is enriched with lively case studies and interview material. It deserves to be widely read.'

PROFESSOR GARETH JONES, *Visiting Professor IE Business School, Madrid, Fellow at London Business School*

'Not only are great leaders first and foremost good human beings, Vlatka's excellent book *Humane Capital*, explains loud and clearly how this can be translated into high performance organisations and above average return. Possibly the best investment you could ever make.'

PAUL POLMAN, *CEO Unilever, Vice-Chair of the Board of the United Nations Global Compact*

'Rich with case studies and stories, Vlatka deftly details the critical importance of a humane and purpose-driven workplace.'

DAN PONTEFRACT, *author of* Open to Think, The Purpose Effice *and* Flat Army, *and Chief Envisioner of TELUS*

'Vlatka Hlupic provides inspiration and direction for those seeking to realize the full potential inside their companies and in society at large. With examples from a wide range of leaders, she shows that high performance begins with a focus on people.'

DEEPA PRAHALAD, *co-author,* Predictable Magic, *Thinkers50 India*

'This book outlines ideas and insights from 59 eminent leaders globally. It implores leaders to adopt humane approach to build their organisations. It enlightens the expectations and aspirations of millennials who constitute predominant workforce globally. It encourages gender-balanced organisations to achieve excellence and effectiveness. I strongly recommend reading it.'

PROFESSOR M.S. RAO, *author of over 40 Books including* 21 Success Sutras for CEOs, *Founder of MSR Leadership Consultants India*

'With rapidly mounting challenges in the social, economic and environmental sectors, Vlatka Hlupic offers with *Humane Capital* a meaningful insight into the world of Leadership in business and non-profit organizations. Vlatka gives guidance with inspiring examples on how and why we need to transform and shift our traditional business by embracing a holistic perspective.'

ALFRED TOLLE, *former director at Google, CEO of Wisdom Together e.V. a non-profit association registered in Germany*

'Vlatka had studied an incredible list of "humane" companies and distilled the practices that more fully engage employees. These are incredible cases and even better insights that can be adapted to any organization. This book reinforces the importance of taking care of people who will take care of customers and others. Very well done!'

DAVE ULRICH, *Professor of Business at the Ross School of Business, University of Michigan, co-founder of The RBL Group,* Wall Street Journal *Business Best-selling author* The Why of Work, *Lifetime Achievement Award recipient from* HR *Magazine, in Thinkers50 Hall of Fame*

"When we think of some of the greatest challenges facing organizations today – disruptors changing the playing field; the gender pay gap; a lack of diversity of thought throughout leadership levels in organizations; the need to resonate with customer needs at the deepest level; the tremendous increase in mental health and stress issues; and five generations of employees to motivate and engage simultaneously – there is no doubt that some organizations are in serious need of transformation. *Humane Capital* provides powerful insights into the approach to follow in order to humanise organizations – as well as the tangible financial rewards that can be gained – from credible leaders who have already done it. As a former CFO, there is no doubt in my mind that – for the sake of continued business performance, relevance and growth – organizations need to be brave in introducing Professor Vlatka's 'big shift', a move that will enable them to create more inspiring working environments that will in turn allow individuals to bring their real selves to work."

TALITA FERREIRA, *CEO Authentic Solutions Ltd, former CFO and HR Director for BMW UK Ltd*

LIST OF TABLES

LIST OF FIGURES

THE DALAI LAMA

FOREWORD

It is my fundamental belief that each of us has a moral responsibility to humanity. I'm convinced that we all possess the potential to contribute to the happiness and welfare of others. Those in the world of business play an important role in our society; it is essential that they assume that role responsibly, especially towards those with whom they engage daily, whose lives depend on them and whom they are dependent on as well.

Though we strive to gratify our desires, satisfaction is attained when we develop self-discipline and more modest needs. Basic human values such as compassion, forgiveness, tolerance which I often refer to as *secular ethics*— secular in the way it is understood in India, impartially respectful of all religions and even the views of those who have none— should be taught within out modern education system. This will enable our young people to take their place in society possessing the tools to assume their responsibilities toward their fellow human beings and to contribute towards a more peaceful and happier world.

Although in business we must consider the need for profit, in today's highly interdependent world we can't be successful if we neglect the concerns of others. In her book *Humane Capital*, Professor Vlatka Hlupic provides strong evidence through powerful case studies that one can do well in business by being good humans. I commend the author for her hard work and hope that her book will achieve its due recognition.

May 28, 2018

PREFACE

Sometimes it seems as though the literature on leadership and the typical workplace have little to do with one another, but if you read a textbook on the benefits of emotionally-intelligent people management and engaged employees aligned with well-directed strategy, the case is indisputable. Many of these books are thoroughly researched, well-written and feature numerous case studies showing how the company that wins the 'Best Employer' gongs also returns more to shareholders.

Yet many workplaces, perhaps the majority, feature listless and reluctant employees in an atmosphere where trust is low and the number of rules and regulations is high. Service is mediocre and the managers are frustrated. In a more rational world, it would be the other way around; the enthused, well managed workers would feature in most organizations. However, one must accept that the world is not perfect and there are dysfunctional, poorly managed workplaces.

My career is, and has been, devoted to working out this puzzle and closing the gap between what the evidence tells us and what is the more typical working experience. My academic and consulting work – my life's work – is about understanding the reasons for this gulf and bringing these two worlds together so that a humane and enlightened workplace becomes the norm, not the rare exception.

I have discovered some of the reasons why the vast library of books on leadership and engagement has not had wider impact. Sometimes, the theory is presented in a way that is difficult to implement; it is rather abstract. Another common feature is that ideas are rather piecemeal; there is an emphasis on an individual leader's ability to motivate and lead teams, but it is not clear how this relates to strategy and the organizational set-up. Or the evidence for the well-organized company is clearly set out, but it isn't obvious how the individual manager can help make it happen when they go into a busy workplace on the following Monday morning.

In my previous book *The Management Shift*, I presented both the evidence for a fundamental shift to a higher-performance way of working, and a practical model that addresses all key aspects of management. It deploys the concept of 'levels' of operation – from Level 1, an extremely disengaged workforce, to Level 5, which features unbounded passion. I drew attention to the particularly significant shift from Level 3, which is orderly and 'command and control', to Level 4, which features highly engaged and enthusiastic workers. It showed how enlightened management, which I referred to as the Emergent Leadership Approach, seeks to optimize performance by encouraging the best out of people and their teams, rather than limiting the worst excesses through rules and regulations. Such empirical evidence of the positive impact of superior leadership behaviour is now supported at the level of social neuroscience and by the mood, behaviour and thoughts of people. These moods are literally infectious – with both positive and negative attributes. They are like neural 'ripples' that flow out from individuals to teams, and sometimes more widely.

High engagement is not enough for good performance; if the strategy is flawed or the systems and resources available within the company are inadequate these issues will present difficulties. Therefore, I merged the engagement model with the 6 Box Leadership Model, which defines the six essential dimensions of organizational management that demand attention. Three relate to people: Relationships, Culture and Individuals. Three relate to processes: Strategy, Systems and Resources. This was based on twenty years of evidence, including research on dozens of successful implementations in the real world.

Reaction to the book, from general readers and especially from managers who have implemented the approach, has been overwhelmingly enthusiastic, especially when people fully engage with the model and start to feel the benefits.

The need for such a change is growing, with a whole generation entering the workplace who have grown up with social media. Millennials have high expectations of an engaging leadership style. They expect communication through conversations, and they do not react well to receiving orders or being given a long list of rules. They expect feedback, encouragement and teamwork.

Yet despite all the evidence and the powerful case studies, the initial conversations I have with people about this approach are often more difficult than I would expect. This has prompted much reflection as to why, which gave me the idea for this follow-up book. In disseminating the ideas around the *Management Shift* model, I have come across a deeper reason as to why progress towards the humane and empowered workplace has not been swift and straightforward; it lies less in the way in which the ideas are put forward, and more with the cultural mindsets that are prevalent throughout society. No matter how strong the evidence, there is extreme scepticism that one can combine humane management and superior shareholder returns, or better value for money in the non-profit sector. Generations of managers have grown up with the belief that there is always a trade-off, that being ruthless or dictatorial is the 'real' way to boost profits and that treating employees well is a luxury. This attitude is often a sub-conscious feeling, not deliberate intent.

My research has found that Level 3 type operations are common, despite being sub-optimal, because these are supported by habits and beliefs that are widespread throughout society. Some common internalised scripts of managers who operate at this level are:

- I should be in charge,

- I should take control,

- I cannot delegate as no one is as capable as I am.

By contrast Level 4 is characterized by thought processes such as:

- I feel energized when interacting with my colleagues,

- I make a difference in the world by serving others,

- I am supportive of my colleagues.

If those promoted to managerial positions have grown up with Level 3 beliefs, they can't easily move to Level 4. The *shift* necessarily takes a conscious effort over a long period of time. The personal challenge of changing one's whole way of operating to a very different manner of thinking, being and doing is considerable if one struggles to believe, deep down, that it will transform performances for the better. This may explain the reluctance to commit to the personal investment necessary, and one can see from the short list above that adopting a Level 4 approach often involves letting go and trusting people. It can feel scary.

This attitudinal issue is the biggest obstacle we face. There is a need, not just for evidence – we have had plenty of that for many years – but for a more fundamental *shift* towards our whole understanding of what the leader's role is, what the purpose of an organization is, as well as understanding of the nature of manager-employee relationships. This means deep conversations in many forums at many levels. Those of us in possession of such valuable evidence – and I have demonstrated in this book there are many of us – have a duty not just to write books and give talks to a management audience, but to engage more widely, give media interviews, TED talks, write letters to newspaper editors, engage in social media, and so on to counter the common perception that the unpleasant workplace is somehow inevitable.

For this book I decided to bring together the distilled wisdom of dozens of leaders to demonstrate the breadth and depth of what is an emerging consensus on enlightened, high-performance workplaces. I have interviewed fifty-eight brilliant individuals, all of whom subscribe to the principles of empowered leadership, and all of whom are successful practitioners in real workplaces. Between them, these interviewees have over 1,700 years of high-achieving experience, and the in-depth interviews generated some 272,000 words of transcript. The result is this book, called *Humane Capital*, a title which succinctly encapsulates the new consensus philosophy that you can do well in business by doing good.

This book has three Parts. In **Part I**, I set out the case for humanizing organizations by encouraging a fundamental shift from a system of orders-based management to a system of empowered workforces. This illustrates how generational changes and advances in technology make the need to shift an imperative for employers, especially those in highly competitive, rapidly changing markets, where failures to adapt and to engage key staff can imperil the organization.

Part II describes in detail the inspirational stories of organizations that have transformed their performance by improving relationships, morale, engagement and skills. It has four chapters, covering respectively the public sector, the corporate sector, SMEs and the voluntary, non-profit sector. They show how the generic principles of the *Management Shift*, the Emergent Leadership and the 6 Box Leadership Model are equally applicable in all types and all sizes of organizations. They show the dramatically positive effects on performance when the *shift* is implemented in full. I draw upon the numerous interviews I carried out which will give detailed information on the case studies.

In **Part III**, I present some overall research data patterns obtained from interviews and I address the wider challenge of creating positive 'ripples' throughout organizations and society. I also describe the risks of *not* taking action and of tolerating stultifying workplaces that have unhappy workers with sub-optimal performances who risk organizational failure. Chapter 6 defines the eight pillars of leveraging humane capital, derived from an analysis of the data that was collected in the research for this book. Chapter 7 addresses the formidable challenge of making the *shift* towards a high-performance workplace. This includes assessments of its huge economic impact and addresses in detail some of the barriers that people may encounter in making the *shift*, with practical advice on how to overcome them. I also discuss the wider impact on society of having happier and more functional workplaces. Further, I discuss the implications of these findings, findings that lead to better leadership behaviours which, together with improved organizational design, leads to superior working experiences and performance. I make the case that we should not baulk at the implications, but instead go out and make the case.

Despite several decades of research that illustrates the benefits of enlightened leadership, in terms of a better organizational climate and superior financial returns, the high-performance workplace is still not the standard. I have spent over twenty years investigating this paradox, and my previous work provides a critique of the reasons why such strong evidence has had limited impact. This has helped me to develop the 'How', a practical approach that any employer can implement. The Management Shift Consulting team and I have been working with many organizations worldwide helping them to implement the future management structure. In this book, I wanted to find out what happens in practice and how organizations go through the *Big Shift* to become more humanized and purpose focused. *Humane Capital* unites theory and practice, the head and the heart, the individual and the organization. It takes the reader through the argument for a radical shift in the business model, shows the successful stories of employers that have made the transition and offers a practical guide for readers to implement.

The ambition for this book is considerable; to be not just practical and insightful, but to leave a lasting legacy for the younger generation and help as many organizations as possible worldwide to become more human, happier and more purposeful workplaces. It also endeavours to facilitate the advancement of the Fourth Industrial Revolution, as Harvard Professor, Mark Esposito puts it succinctly:

Vlatka's contribution pushes an open door in the direction of how the Fourth Industrial Revolution envisions the role of organizations in the 21st century: Maximizing Human Well-Being.

Throughout the book, I use terms *the shift, The Big Shift, a management shift and The Management Shift*® interchangeably – they all refer to the *shift* from old ways of management that were based on hierarchical command and control. The new ways are based on humane, people and purpose focused ways of management.

There is also a personal story behind this book. A few weeks after the successful launch of *The Management Shift* in November 2014, I started thinking about what could I do in 2015 that would mark my forthcoming big birthday, which had to be related to my passion, mission and life purpose. Climbing a mountain, running a marathon or abseiling would challenge me for sure, but I didn't find any of these ideas sufficiently exciting, and they lacked purpose. So I got the idea of interviewing fifty inspirational leaders in 2015 to mark my fiftieth birthday, and share the stories about how they shifted their organizations to Level 4 or how they are helping other organizations to *shift* to Level 4.

The original book title I chose was *Leaders50*, as a complement to Thinkers50.[1] Thinkers50 write about management, while leaders read about management and implement ideas. As I was delivering one of many keynote talks about *The Management Shift*® in 2015, I kept meeting more and more inspirational leaders at these events and, through my network, I just couldn't stop doing these interviews. So I continued these interviews into 2016, going beyond the fifty interviewees I originally envisaged. In the end, I interviewed fifty-eight leaders who brought to this project a collective wisdom obtained over many years of combined leadership experience – and these interviews

---

[1] http://thinkers50.com/

provided a huge amount of qualitative data! I read all interview transcripts several times; it was not easy to decide which parts should go in the book because there were so many inspirational quotes in transcripts. I was literally spoilt for choice!

Interviewing these leaders was one of the most enjoyable research projects I have ever conducted. I have had many eureka and inspirational moments during these interviews, getting validation and confirmation for my own research from these inspirational leaders. In the process of writing this book I decided to change the book title to *Humane Capital* as this better describes what the book is about.

The main image on the book cover is a butterfly with eight stripes in the shape of heart. The butterfly is a symbol for *The Management Shift®* brand, representing emergence, transformation and the *Big Shift* toward more humane workplaces. The eight stripes represent the eight pillars that leverage the *Humane Capital*, identified from this research (as described in Chapter 6). The shape of the heart represents compassion associated with word *humane*.

The origami theme in *The Management Shift®* brand represents the holistic approach to my work, a combination of western science and eastern philosophy. Finally, number 8, in numerology and eastern philosophy, represents infinity and the abundance this book is trying to bring to its readers.

On a personal level, this book is another gift from me to humanity on my quest to live my purpose, work on something much bigger than me and make this world a better place. I wrote it for practitioners, academics and students to provide hope and show the direction and possibilities available, and to provide practical research-based advice on how organizations can be, should be and could be. This work aims to be a change agent in today's world, which is replete with business, economic, political and social challenges.

I believe that we can achieve success and happiness when we fulfil our most authentic and truthful expression of ourselves as human beings. We spend a majority of our adult life working, so it is very important that we spend this time doing something we love and make these working years meaningful and special. Follow our true calling, do what we were born to do, work to live not live to work, and intertwine our lives with work in a creative, empowering, fulfilling and fun way – this is all possible in humane workplaces with Level 4/5 culture.

Many of my interviewees said that going through the *Big Shift* was a choice between happiness and an unfulfilling life; even between life and death. It is priceless, unlimited and profoundly important. Anyone can create ripples to make workplaces more humane, engaging and fulfilling, while at the same time become more productive and profitable. Organizations can do well by doing good. I hope that this book will inspire you to start creating your own ripples and make this world a better place for the future generations. The choice is yours and the time is now!

ACKNOWLEDGEMENTS

Writing and launching my previous book "The Management Shift" was a life changing experience. This enabled me to connect with tens of thousands of people via social media, spread the ripples globally with my ideas and meet thousands of people during more than 50 keynote talks in the first couple of years since the book launch. Soon after the launch of "The Management Shift" book, an idea for the follow up book was born and I started working on interviews for this book.

This book is a result of interactions and discussions with many inspirational people, and I am hugely grateful to everyone who has helped on this journey in any way. First of all, I would like to thank my beloved children Ana Helena and Tomislav for their unconditional love, support, inspiration and patience with my often preoccupied mind. Working on a quest to make this world a better place would not have been possible without support and understanding from my closest family. Again, I wish to thank my forever missed late parents Helena and Vladimir for their legacy, for instilling persistence, love, courage and integrity in me and for unconditional love and wonderful support I received from them during my education and an earlier part of my career.

Many friends and colleagues have provided inspiration, support and guidance on the journey of writing this book and I thank everyone from the bottom of my heart. A special thank you goes to interviewees who have given enthusiastically their time and support for this project: Chris Shern, Doug Kirkpatrick, Kevin O'Brien, Jack Bergstrand, Marshall Goldsmith, Celine Shillinger, Peter Cheese, Ann Francke, Richard Barrett, Vineet Nayar, Anders Bouvin, Avivah Wittenberg-Cox, Ry Morgan, Mick Yates, Steven Denning, Sir Paul Judge, Dana Denis-Smith, Rob Noble, Paul Polman, Geoff McDonald,

Charlie Isaacs, John Stepper, Paul Excell, Rob Wirszycz, Charles Elvin, Graeme Nuttall OBE, Martin Donnelly, Simon Fowler, Martin Mackay, Michael Goethe, Paul Dolman, Helen Walton, Stelio Verzera, Jack Hubbard, Nigel Girling, Jules Goddard, Jos de Blok, Simon La Fosse, David MacLeod OBE, Dame Fiona Woolf CBE, Brian Walker, Tom Rippin, Anita Krohn Traaseth, Paul Little, Rick Wartzman, Gerwin Schuring, Richard Straub, Arie de Geus, Karin Tenelius, Stephen Ball, Lord David Evans, Caroline Minshell, Justin Packshaw, Ajaz Ahmed, Sam Kelly, Kalyan Madabhushi, Curtis Carlson and Michael Jenkins.

I am grateful to His Holiness The Dalai Lama for offering to write a Foreword for this book, and members of His Holiness' Office for their help in this process. I would like to thank Christopher Cudmore for his initial interest in this book, Ian Hallsworth and Emily Bedford of Bloomsbury Publishing for commissioning this book and supporting the production and book launch; Katie Lawrence for all her help with book production, my editorial adviser Philip Whiteley for helping with editing of the draft of this book; Merv Honeywood and Giles Herman for managing the production of this book; Neil Burnip for help with book editing in production stage; Kealey Rigden and Emily Crowley Wroe for help with book marketing; Vladimir Bobovsky for help with graphic design; Debbie Willis and Rod Willis for help with data analysis; Jenny Ropper, Ben Walker and other journalists for enthusiastically helping to spread my ideas; Jan Schapira, Audrey Chapman and Emma Turner for help with marketing, Gordan Bosnjak and Alec Saiko for website development; members of The Management Shift team for their support: Steven D'Souza, Kenny Elpick, Matt Hancock, Gary Hunt, Peter Neville Lewis, Annemarie O'Connor, Inge Relph, Alfred Tolle, Paul Turner, Rachel Whitehouse, Avivah Wittenberg Cox and Talita Ferreira. I am grateful to Shazir Kabir Sheikh and her colleagues from Herman Miller for hosting and sponsoring the book launch and to Nicholas Jarrold, Peter Elborn and their colleagues from the British-Croatian Society for offering to organise the book launch, and for support from his Excellency Igor Pokaz, Croatian Ambassador in the United Kingdom.

A special gratitude goes to: Richard Straub, Rick Wartzman, Kenneth Mikkelsen, Martin Mackay, Graeme Nuttall, Celine Shillinger, Geoff McDonald and Dawna Jones for connecting me with some of the interviewees; colleagues from Birkbeck College at University of London and from Westminster Business School for their support for my work; Fran Kruc, Geoffrey Wolfson, Peter Starbuck, Jamie Hutchinson and other volunteers from the Drucker Society London for spreading the positive ripples I started.

I am grateful for all endorsements received for this book. A special gratitude goes to: Julian Birkinshaw, David Burkus, Simon Caulkin, Sangeet Paul Choudary, Subir Chowdhury, Sir Cary Cooper, Rajeeb Dey, Oleg Elshin, Mark Esposito, Talita Ferreira, Sunil Gupta, Phil James, Gareth Jones, Paul Polman, Deepa Prahalad, Dan Pontefract, M.S. Rao, Alfred Tolle and Dave Ulrich.

Last, but not least, I am very grateful to many other special people that have touched my life journey in different ways, helped me to shift my consciousness and keep pursuing my purpose. A special gratitude goes to: Adeeb, Ahlya, Alemka, Annetta, Amina, Amanda, Arci, Bobi, Boris, Boza, Bozhena, Cathy, Chad, Chris, Dane, David, Duska, Flora, Fran, Francika, Eileen, Iman, Jack, Jane, Jasna, Jennifer, Jo, Jules, Karen L, Karen B, Katarina C, Katarina Z, Kellie, Koraljka, Laura, Layla, Lidia, Kristina, Mamdouh, Marcus, Marianne, Mario, Mladen, Mira, Mirela, Mirna, Nada, Nathalie, Nuno, Paul, Philip, Ray, Renata, Sajda, Sally, Sasa A, Sasa M, Shant, Shirley, Snjezana, Stewart, Stipe, Sue, Susan, Susannah, Suzana, Tatjana, Tereza, Vanda and Zrinka. A special gratitude goes to my dear friend and personal development mentor Baroness Lidia Antunes-Frederico, whose wisdom, compassion and love for humanity have been hugely inspiring and instrumental for my own shifts in consciousness and reaching new levels of achievement. Last, but not least, I would like to thank the source of divine inspiration for my work.

Thank you all!

PART I

WHY DO WE NEED TO HUMANIZE ORGANIZATIONS

1

The traditional business model is broken!

KEY INSIGHTS FROM THIS CHAPTER

- A dehumanizing approach to management based on a static concept of deploying people as resources is no longer fit for purpose.
- The need to update each company's business model is made more acute in this volatile world with its rapid technological and demographic changes. Changes must be made so as to provide for the expectations of the millennial generation.
- Research now strongly supports empowering leadership styles, encompassing all aspects of business strategies and processes, as well as innovation and design.
- Presently, only a minority of workplaces can be categorized as being passionate and high-performance, and they have a significant competitive advantage.
- *Shifting* to a high-performance culture means a comprehensive cultural change for some organizations, not just an incremental increase in employee engagement.
- There is a practical, proven approach for *shifting* to higher levels of performance.

Business as usual is not an option anymore

Although the evidence for a high-engagement, high-performance workplace is strong, sometimes it still feels as if striving for this enviable state of affairs is an optional extra that need not be introduced. As noted in the preface to this book, it isn't easy to implement the required improvements. In my recent work I have come across powerful trends which suggest that many organizations have little choice but to reform and adapt. If they do not become more nimble, adaptable, equitable and empowering they will lose out in the competitive struggle. I shall discuss some of these trends in this chapter, and I shall also refer to technological and demographic changes.

This is not simply about a war for talent, it is a fundamental *shift*. The dehumanizing business model that many of us grew up with in the late twentieth century, which always had limitations, has become increasingly unviable in today's business environment. Management involves choice. If you choose not to prioritize the empowerment and motivation of those people who report to you, then you are choosing to disempower and demotivate them, and this can be done at the subconscious level. So the question that arises is, how does pursuing sub-optimal empowerment and motivation for the teams that deliver your services help you achieve your objectives? In a competitive marketplace your customers will be better served by employees who are energized in the delivery of their products and services, and these are continually developed and updated by a highly innovative team.

In my earlier book, *The Management Shift*,[1] I described the concept of different levels of individual mindset and the corresponding organizational culture in an Emergent Leadership Model. These levels start at Level 1, which is negative and seriously dysfunctional, through to Level 5, which is unbounded and passionate. (See Figure 1.1 and Table 1.1) Each level is characterized by specific thinking patterns, behaviour, language used, leadership style and organizational outcomes. For example, Level 1 is characterized by apathy or destructive behaviour while Level 2 is characterized by the reluctant behaviour of employees who only do the minimum necessary to be paid. There is a particularly significant shift from Level 3, which is ordered and bureaucratic, to Level 4, which is where highly-engaged and inventive performance begins. The keywords and phrases at this level are: trust, transparency, purpose, collaboration, passion, giving back to society and having fun when working. Level 5 is where passionate people combine creatively to make that difference.

As described in the preface, the upward move to Levels 4 and 5 is uneven, but what is emerging is a cadre of high-performing businesses that operate at Levels 4 and 5 who are pulling away from the rest of the economy. A report by Deloitte found that only twelve per cent of the US workforce operates at a passionate level and it is they who meet or exceed performance expectations. The report also notes that the remaining eighty-eight per cent of the working population operates at the sub-optimal level, though many exhibit some elements of passion and engagement.[2] However, a more recent Gallup international survey, which provided a comparison with my earlier studies, revealed a slight increase in worker passion and a drop in the level of disengagement.

The United States and Canada scored best of all in the poll, recording twenty-nine per cent of employees as being highly-engaged.[3] Another study revealed a similar picture, with twenty-eight per cent of the North American workforce being identified as purpose-driven. The benefits that these motivated workforces bring to their organizations include, inter alia, a twenty per cent increase in the probability of an employee staying with their employer for two years or more, while fifty-four per cent are more likely to feel that their work has had some impact.[4] The overall picture that emerged was that, in most economies, a minority of the workforce was responsible for the majority of passion, innovation and added economic value. This is a finding that ought to awake the interest of policy makers as well as business managers.

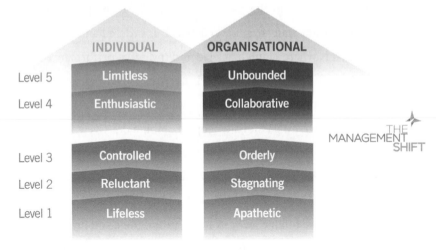

FIGURE 1.1 *Five Levels of the Emergent Leadership Model.*

TABLE 1.1 *A description of the five Levels of the Emergent Leadership Model*

LEVEL	SYMBOL	DESCRIPTION
Level 1		The mindset is *Lifeless*, the culture is *Apathetic*. Not much gets done at this level. The culture is based on fear. Employees are isolated and disengaged.
Level 2		The mindset is *Reluctant*, the culture is *Stagnating*. People do the minimum they can just to get a paycheck. Leadership is autocratic. There is a blame culture and employees feel overwhelmed.
Level 3		The mindset is *Controlled* and the organizational culture is *Orderly*. Leadership style is based on the traditional command and control. Employees are micromanaged. They do what they are told to do.

THE MANAGEMENT SHIFT / THE BIG SHIFT MANAGEMENT^{THE} SHIFT®

| Level 4 | | The mindset *is Enthusiastic*, the culture is *Collaborative*. Emergent leadership is implemented. There is a strong teamwork ethos. Integrity, passion, purpose, transparency, accountability and a caring culture are embedded at this level. |
| Level 5 | | The mindset is *Limitless* and the culture *Unbounded*. Anything can be achieved at this level. Teams work on breakthrough innovations that solve big problems. |

Source: Vlatka Hlupic (2014), *The Management Shift – How to Harness the Power of People and Transform Your Organisation for Sustainable Success*, Palgrave Macmillan

Organizations face unprecedented challenges

Life has never been predictable, but, arguably, the level of volatility facing modern organizations is increasing. This instability has been the subject of much research and has become known by the acronym VUCA. This stands for Volatility, Uncertainty, Complexity and Ambiguity. These helpful distinctions, made between the different dimensions of external risk, help management teams prepare.[5] A succinct summary appears in Table 1.2

In the early twenty-first century we experienced the rapid industrialization of emerging economies and the deepening and widening of global trade. This was facilitated and accelerated by the use of the internet. Yet these largely positive, benign forces were followed by the great banking and financial crash of 2008 to 2009, the aftermath of which still persists. This aftermath featured the introduction of unprecedented financial stimuli such as quantitative easing, ultra-low interest rates, high government debt, austerity programmes and, in some regions, resurgent nationalism and conflict.

TABLE 1.2 *A definition of VUCA world*

Volatility	This refers to a known external variable with a significant impact on a business that is highly unpredictable and beyond the control of a single enterprise. A recent example is the price of oil, which fell from in excess of $100 per barrel to around $30 in the period 2014 to 2016.
Uncertainty	This refers to a situation when the event's basic cause and effect are not known. Change might be possible but it is not certain. An example might be the launch of the new product by competitor, where its impact on the business and market is not certain.
Complexity	This situation has multiple variable factors that affect outcomes. An example would be trading a complex service internationally, but under different regulatory regimes.
Ambiguity	Causal effects are all but impossible to ascertain – the context is wholly new and there are no precedents. An example is entering a new market with a new technology that is potentially disruptive and untested in that market.

Source: https//hbr.org/2014/01/what-vuca-really-means-for-you

One thing is clear, however, a rigid, rules-based, dehumanized workplace is ill-suited to react positively to any dimension of the VUCA world. In a VUCA world, where technology and customer preferences change rapidly and your workforce is comprised of highly-skilled and informed people who are in demand from other employers, the need for innovation and motivation is relentless.

There are clear warning signs that the generally accepted business model and the teaching of management theory has not kept pace with these changing demands. Corporate life expectancy alone has plummeted seventy-five per cent in the past fifty years.[6] Some of this may be inevitable given the nature of our VUCA world, but this statistic provides a stark warning that one should guard against complacency in management education and leadership philosophy. Many of the studies that illustrate the advantages of a high-engagement, high-performance workforce reveal that this is still a minority habit (as noted in the preface). Emergent leadership is now essential, not an optional extra. However, the starting point for many organizations is low.

Shifting from command and control to humanized management

The biggest improvement in performance does not come from simply improving employee engagement and skills, but from a broader improvement in distributed leadership. This involves adopting a different mindset, as well as using different tactics and approaches. One must view the company not as a set of resources, but as a vital community with complex, interconnected constituencies of skilled teams.

In my work with clients I have found that it is difficult for them to make a change in mindset if they themselves have grown up in a Level 3 command and control culture. The taken-for-granted assumptions about management and leadership that one has at Level 3 – I must be in control, leadership is just giving orders, etc. – are often ingrained in those individuals who have been promoted to their first managerial post. Consequently, it is only through in-depth and reflective discussions about working practices that one can begin to change both their mindsets and their behaviour, and thereafter company policies and procedures. It is then necessary to monitor the impact these changed mindsets and behaviours have on the team.

In the past, a move towards a more empowering leadership style was backed by intuition, common sense and, perhaps, some empirical evidence. Recently the evidence base has grown in strength and depth. As well as using empirical research to identify positive impacts, we can also point to findings from the emerging discipline of social neuroscience. Researchers on emotional intelligence, Daniel Goleman and Richard Boyatzis noted in the Harvard Business Review article, *Social Intelligence and the Biology of Leadership*, 2008, that a deeper understanding of neuroscience has revealed many of the subconscious dynamics by which we predict the moods and attitudes of those around us. The salient discovery was that certain things that leaders do, specifically exhibiting empathy and becoming attuned to the moods of others, affects their own brain chemistry and that of their followers. Indeed, researchers have found that the leader-follower dynamic is not a case of two or more independent brains reacting consciously or subconsciously to one another, rather the individual minds become, in a sense, fused into a single consciousness.[7]

Goleman and Boyatzis further added that a recently classified group of brain cells known as mirror neurons operate as a form of *neural Wi-Fi* for people in social contexts. When we pick up upon someone else's emotions and/ or actions, our mirror neurons reproduce those same emotions. What occurs in teams of people is a much deeper and more physical experience than the traditional concepts of leadership and followership. Many people experience this deep bonding in a sports team or when playing music together, where the shared experience is intense and uplifting. What we have learned recently is that this also occurs in those high-performing work teams who operate at Levels 4 and 5.

Combined, this mass of evidence on high-performance workplaces and the effect that neural connectivity has on people within the group completely transforms our understanding of the managerial role. It is beginning to transform the way in which we select and develop leaders throughout the breadth of an organization. It is beginning to transform the way in which we communicate, motivate and relate to other people. This transformation was once regarded as no more than a supporting role and was, supposedly, of lesser importance than setting strategy, developing products and understanding finance. However, it is now considered to be a central tenet of management philosophy and, moreover, it is the key to improving the performance of teams and, thereafter, the whole organization. The result is that performance changes from sub-optimal to stellar – and the stories in the latter part of this book provide ample examples of this.

Changing demographics: what do millennials want?

An entire generation that has grown up with social media and internet trading is now entering the workplace. Their expectations for connectivity at work and elsewhere are of an order that is entirely different to that of earlier generations. They often prioritize work content, work-life balance and a sense of purpose ahead of maximizing earnings. In 2015, this generation was defined as those aged between the ages of eighteen and thirty-four. While some attributes of a healthy workplace – fairness, good communication, career opportunities – are appreciated by all generations, there are strong indications that millennials have certain traits that are worth paying attention to. They attracted the attention of the US publication, *100 Best Workplaces for Millennials*. According to a report in *Fortune* magazine, 'These workplaces exhibit strong, open, two-way communication; a high tolerance for risk-taking; high levels of cooperation and support among employees; and reduced roadblocks to innovation, such as internal politics.'[8]

The report commends the Boston Consulting Group, one of the companies that featured in the top 100, who reformed its approach to recruitment and training so as to reflect the preferences of the younger generation. It became obvious that millennials had grown up with social media and they placed a high value on information from contemporaries, so Boston incorporated peer relationships into its recruiting strategy. It also gave millennials the opportunity to work pro bono with high profile client projects.

The UK's Management 2020 report, launched at the Houses of Parliament in July 2014, included testimony from young business leaders as well as findings on generational differences. The millennials, it found, were very likely to switch jobs early in their careers and look for meaning as well as financial reward. They were highly entrepreneurial, with more than one quarter seriously considering setting up their own business. In oral evidence to the Parliamentary Commission that produced the report, Ry Morgan, a young entrepreneur, said, 'Space and autonomy instil a high level of responsibility, trust and authenticity. That's how I would have liked to have been managed, and I like to think that's how I manage others.'[9]

A further complication to managing generational change comes from the increased lifespans of people combined with the disappointing returns from many pension funds. Because of these economic pressures, this means that many older people stay in work longer or, having once retired, they then return to the workplace. Some workplaces now employ four generations of employees, with ages ranging from nineteen to seventy-five.

The unstoppable force of disruptive technologies

New technologies have been disrupting business models for centuries, leading to either product obsolescence or changed roles for pre-existing products. Some of the most recent technical developments have been much less obvious than, say, the very visible replacement of the horse and carriage by motorized transport over a century ago. One of the largest of these recent disruptions has been the trend to achieve the integration of front office (contact centre) operations with back office (data processing and administrative) functions.

Many of the most successful companies are those that handle the customer interface rather than own or produce the end product. It was observed that Uber, the world's largest taxi company, owns no vehicles; Facebook, the world's most popular media owner, creates no content; Alibaba, the most valuable retailer, has no inventory; and Airbnb, the world's largest accommodation provider, owns no real estate.[10] In an interview for this book, Anita Krohn Traaseth, former head of technology giant HP Norway, observed:

> Technology is changing the way we do things. It is going to change the risk perspective, security perspective, the control perspective, and big data. One of the first things I first did was to put the digital officer straight into a top management position. You need to have technological expertise at the very top. It's very, very important. I think we should probably stop talking about technology as software and hardware. We should talk about the digital shift, what it's doing to our workplaces, what it's doing to the way that our customers now interact with us and what it's doing to the way we are delivering our services. We need to talk about how the work life [balance] is changing, because it's changing everything.

Another complication is that change is neither linear nor predictable. Take, for example, e-books. Between 2010 and 2013 there was strong growth in the sale of e-readers, while the market for printed books was challenging. According to a report by the Association of American Publishers and the Book Industry Study Group, sales of e-books increased from six per cent to fifteen per cent of the US market between 2010 and 2011.[11] However, by Christmas 2014 the sales growth of printed books had returned. The UK retailer, Waterstones, recorded book sales as being five per cent higher than the year before, while there was a sharp decrease in the sale of e-readers.[12]

The disruption that a new technology introduces may completely replace old technology (email and text replaced the telegram), or the new technology may become a new element in a diverse range of products or services (TV and the internet alongside radio). The point for organizations and their leadership is that they have to be prepared for this disruption and they must be prepared to engage the unexpected twists that occur along the way.

Another example of disruptive technology is 3D printing. Again, we face unpredictable dynamics. When compared to injection moulding or the tooling of components, this is a completely different approach to standard manufacturing processes. Instead of starting with a raw material and moulding it to the required shape and strength, the item is built up by adding numerous layers of compound until it conforms to the pre-set computer-generated design. This is also known as additive manufacturing. Waste material from this form of manufacturing is effectively zero. It took just eighteen months for 3D printing to replace conventional manufacturing in the hearing aid sector. Whereas this technology is most suitable for customized items such as hearing aids and dental implants, it is increasingly being used by major companies to manufacture other components. According to a 2014 PwC survey of more than 100 manufacturing companies, eleven per cent had switched to volume production of 3D printed parts and components. This list included jet engine manufacturers and the makers of unmanned aerial vehicles.[13] Although the impact of 3D printing will likely be considerable, it is unlikely that it will replace conventional manufacturing for the mass production of standard components in the foreseeable future.[14]

The dislocation caused to the manufacturing sector may sometimes resemble publishing, where different technologies coexist and evolve in parallel. From a leadership point of view the salient question becomes, 'Is your business going to have its entire way of operating changed completely within the next eighteen months? Or changed partially? Or, instead of an eighteen month period, say, in a four-year period?' There is no way of knowing for sure, but those organizations that are operating at Level 4 and above, those that are nimble, innovative and highly engaged, will respond more quickly and more positively to change than those at Level 3.

Gender-balanced organizations achieve more

From the field of cognitive psychology there is increasing evidence of the dangers of *groupthink*, a narrow perspective dominating a company or team's operations and strategy. It is well documented that this was a major contributor to the irresponsible levels of risk taken by the banks, which led to the financial crash in 2008. This was exacerbated by the adrenaline rush of nearly all-male and highly competitive teams who were all from a similar background, and who made the same limited assumptions about risk.[15]

One outcome of this, which was reinforced by the findings of social neuroscience research, strongly supports the case for more gender-balanced leadership teams. Indeed, a diversity of background generally promotes better decision-making. A summary of this research, published in *Scientific American* in 2014, lists the benefits. The body of researchers was eclectic: organizational scientists, psychologists, sociologists, economists and demographers. The dimensions of social diversity encompassed race, ethnicity, gender and sexual orientation. The researchers concluded that the greater the diversity, the greater the capacity for innovation. This diversity held an advantage over homogeneous groups when solving complex, non-routine problems because people from different backgrounds bring new information and a new outlook when looking at problems from different perspectives. They are better able to ask penetrating questions about taken-for-granted assumptions than those groups who come from a similar background. Being challenged also encourages people to prepare better, to anticipate alternative viewpoints and to agree that reaching a consensus takes effort.[16] In a similar manner, learning a different language enables one to look at the world from a different viewpoint, while enhancing cognition.

In Norway, the appointment of a high proportion of women board members has been mandatory since 2008. The effects seem to have been beneficial for the businesses concerned, as well as for these career women and the wider society. One study, published in *The Atlantic*, reported, 'The directors

I interviewed believed that women were more likely than men to thoroughly deliberate and evaluate risks.' Women, in their view, showed a greater propensity to monitor firm management.[17]

Other countries are following suit. In the UK, an initiative by the government to achieve more balance resulted in the doubling of the number of women board members, from about twelve per cent to around twenty-five per cent during the period 2010 to 2015, with further improvements targeted.[18] Avivah Wittenberg-Cox, CEO of gender consultancy 20-First, observed:

> I think the issue today is [that] most of these large organizations have been built and designed by men for men. But not all men, just a particular subset of men who are heavily IQ task-oriented, and not so EQ. They are very driven on a particular set of leadership criteria that are now obsolete in terms of what the next generation wants, what the customers want, what stakeholders want, what governments want and what the country needs. I think there's a bit of a disconnect there, but there's a self-fulfilling issue going on inside organizations.

Avivah does not believe that it is an issue of men versus women, but there is a small subset of men that are continually preferred by the systems they created themselves. Gender balance is a way to cut through that, it brings with it different people with different value systems, different leadership styles and different ways of *being*. It brings in a lot of women and men who don't behave like the small subset of men described above. She added:

> So I think most women do not fit or agree with the current system's values, approaches and styles, so either organizations change or the women leave. Gender balance is a very easy mix. I would compare it to the canary and the lion. If there are women, it's because mindsets have shifted; if there aren't women, it's because they haven't. It's that simple.

The key to the productivity challenge: people

In many leading economies, levels of productivity have not been able to keep pace. The conventional wisdom used to be that with investment in infrastructure and skills, maximization of automation and other technological developments, and the development of open markets with good competition rules, innovation and productivity would increase. This hasn't always happened and economists are somewhat puzzled.

My research and that of others in the emerging field of empowerment and enlightened leadership points to an explanation. In the past, when Level 3 ways of thinking were prevalent in the economy, it was assumed that efforts to humanize the workplace were in conflict with the quest for an orderly and efficient production line. Generations of managers had grown up with the *Fordist* assumption that the worker was merely a replaceable resource and that attending to their ambitions and morale was a distraction or an indulgence. Conformity to Level 3 thinking was widespread and, in discussions on economics, it was rare to see the *Fordist* belief challenged.

We can now confidently conclude from our research that the reason why productivity hasn't improved is not that managers and organizations haven't been trying, it is because they have been trying with a flawed approach. The flaw lies partly in the preponderance of a limiting belief, i.e. the tacit assumption that an ordered Level 3 way of working is the most efficient. What the research now shows is that this approach is far from efficient. The outcomes were sub-optimal at best and, worse still, they tended to result in the sub-optimal use of technology as well as people. As Anita Krohn Traaseth, Chief Executive of Innovasjon Norway, observed:

> You cannot digitalize work processes if they don't work. You must fix them first otherwise you are doing something worse, you are digitalizing bad processes. One must look at the culture, the work processes and the needs

of the customer first, then digitalize. When you digitalize do it stepwise, otherwise projects that are big and expensive will fail.

Chapter 2, which focuses on transforming service and performance in the public sector, features a full interview with Anita Krohn Traaseth and a case study on Innovasjon Norway.

The research presented in this book, in *The Management Shift* and elsewhere, overturns the assumptions that have led to the sub-optimal use of resources, including technological resources. The case studies presented in this book demonstrate how productivity can be lifted to higher levels by energizing and empowering the workforce with breakthrough, successful concepts such as crowd-sourcing and self-organization. Understanding that humanizing the workplace helps rather than hinders productivity is, potentially, a huge breakthrough for economic theorists and policy-makers, as well as organizational leaders. That is clearly the conclusion that my research and the research of others points towards. What is underestimated is the extent to which this approach constitutes a different mindset and a different set of priorities.

Introducing a practical guide

This book, and *The Management Shift* before it, chronicles some of the major changes in markets and society, together with the implications this has for leaders and managers. These publications also record how our collective knowledge about the nature of the organization as a living, organic entity has gone through fundamental changes in recent years.

This book calls for managers and business schools to respond in a manner that is proportionate to the scale of these changes and to the significance of these research findings. A response of simply making minor adjustments to the standard business model and leadership style is not sufficient. The evidence is clear, but the challenge is multi-dimensional both for individuals and organizations.

The response must include strategy and processes as well as people and relationships. It's at the level of neurons, i.e. the individual mindset, and the level of society. A fundamental *shift* is required. *The Management Shift's* added value lies in providing the answer to the question, *how*? It provides a proven and practical programme to enhance the leadership and management skills that are required to effect this transformation. This includes encouraging diversity and bridging cultural gaps. It is an approach in which all aspects of the complex, living entity that forms the organization are understood as being inter-related; in which relationships, emotions, morale and engagement are properly acknowledged as powerful forces. The remainder of this book sets out practical challenges with a view to making them as easily implementable as possible. The challenge is complex, but it is not impossible. It is multi-dimensional, but is capable of being divided into clear tasks, habits and learning disciplines. Many organizations have profited from making the journey, as we shall discover later.

 SEVEN REFLECTION POINTS FROM THIS CHAPTER

1 Is your company in the vanguard of innovation within its sector or is it struggling to catch up?
2 Do business leaders and others within the organization create space for scenario planning and other forms of deep strategic discussion that will enable the organization to stay abreast of technological, political and demographic changes?
3 Are some parts of the business more effective than others? If this is the case, what efforts are being made to understand the cause of these difference? Do you have plans to close these gaps? Do you propose to lift the performance of the weaker areas?

4 Is your organization diverse and internationally aware, or is it broadly male and dominated by one national culture? Are you aware of the advantages of greater openness and diversity?

5 Are you paying attention to your employees' mindsets as well as organizational changes? For example, is there a move toward delegated leadership in cultures where many people expect a command and control way of operating?

6 Do you consider employee engagement, culture and relationships when designing technological upgrades or a business restructure, or when devising personal leadership development programs?

7 Are you aware of the management needs of the new generation of employees?

PART II

HUMANE CAPITAL INTERVIEWS:

WHAT ARE THE BEST PRACTICES THAT EMERGE FROM HUMANIZED ORGANIZATIONS

2

Winning strategies: how the public sector achieves more with less

KEY INSIGHTS FROM THIS CHAPTER

- Leadership and employee engagement are vital for boosting productivity in the public sector.
- New technology will not improve services without effective management. Poor implementation can harm productivity.
- Moving from a Level 3 to a Level 4 performance is essential if the public sector is to do more with less, but this considerable challenge needs to be addressed in terms of mindset, leadership style and organizational structure.
- Reform is best when integrated. New organizations will not be effective with Level 3 mindsets.

Better public services in an age of austerity

The scale of the debt crisis that emerged in the period 2008 to 2009 meant that the public purse had to be tightened in all major economies. Arguably, this has been taken too far in some places and there has been much debate, especially in Europe, over the extent to which public expenditure should be reduced, and over the pace and scale of change. Does this mean that a reduction in public provision is inevitable? The findings from *The Management Shift* indicate that there is a huge untapped potential within the workforce to effect service improvements without increasing budgets, but only if we move from a Level 3 to a Level 4 mindset. Given that doing more with less is likely to be on the agenda for some time to come, the value of such a move becomes self-evident.

Higher performance and productivity is as important in the public sector as it is in the private sector. In discussions on policy, the quest to improve productivity is often dominated by calls for investment in infrastructure, skills and technology, always assuming that a linear relationship exists between investment and better service and productivity. However, as discussed in Chapter 1, these assumptions neglect the fact that some organizations have far higher productivity than others, even where the skill levels and technology investments are similar and all have the same infrastructure.

My own research,[1] corroborated by many other studies, clearly shows that the calibre of leadership and management is the differentiating factor. As an example, take the period 2003 to 2008 when the UK saw large increases in public spending and huge modernizing initiatives to bring public services into the digital age. The results were somewhat capricious. Some of the automation initiatives were costly failures due to the failure to train key parts of the workforce. Poorly planned project management or over-simplifications of the task in hand must also take their share of the blame, as must the weak procurement processes that led to contractor overpayments.

A major study concluded that the cost to the public purse of these mistakes ran into hundreds of millions of pounds and that nearly all of the cost lay in managerial failings, not policy errors.[2] Let's reflect on that. Increased budgets, including huge investments in automation and infrastructure, actually reduced productivity in some parts of the public sector. To someone schooled in Level 3 thinking, this is a puzzle. From the *Management Shift* perspective, it is perfectly logical. The leadership and management dimension had been downplayed, or overlooked completely. From errors in project management during the era when budgets were more generous to the challenges posed in the subsequent years of austerity, we learned the same lesson – the calibre of leadership and empowerment is key.

As an example of good practice in improving public sector productivity, later in this chapter I shall describe how Innovasjon Norway cut the time taken to approve start-up grants for entrepreneurs from sixty days to four days. This was done by transforming both the management and the culture, dimensions that are too often absent from policy discussions. Innovations that are emerging in the public sector, e.g. the creation of self-organized teams and other participative endeavours, have created an increased number of opportunities to improve productivity. This chapter highlights these findings with practical examples that can be used to influence not-for-profit employees everywhere.

Inspirational stories from public sector employers

Department for Business, Innovation and Skills – UK

As the former Permanent Secretary of the Department for Business, Innovation and Skills in the UK, Sir Martin Donnelly's encouragement of *The Management Shift* has had a multiplier effect on the UK's wider economy. Not only can the Department itself move forward to Level 4 ways of thinking and performance, it can now nurture the same approach in businesses throughout the economy. Moving to Level 4 is 'almost [like] buying a licence to go on operating in the twenty-first century'. He added:

> We play a big outreach role to all sorts of businesses in their sectors in terms of support schemes for high-tech businesses, start-ups, or work with UK companies on trade and investments on exports. We connect with a lot of

businesses and as well as challenging them on their use of technology, their skills base or their analysis of new markets, we can do more and say, 'Have you looked at the way you run yourselves? As well as upgrading to the latest machinery or software, have you upgraded your management and leadership skills by using these sorts of techniques?' There is no doubt that poor management and leadership skills can place a huge constraint on the success of an organization, whether in the private, public or third sectors. If an organization cannot move away from command and control (while retaining its focus on the essential disciplines that impact on safety and other issues), [it will struggle].

Hierarchy was never any more than a means to an end, the organization has to change so that it serves its own people – people who are often the most junior, but who are the most outward-facing in their dealings with customers, clients, suppliers etc. I think the old model doesn't have a future. So yes, we must move in this direction – in different ways for different types of organizations – and [toward] collaborative teamwork. That's the only way that allows you to add sustainable value today.

Creating such a positive culture is also enormously helpful in terms of attracting and retaining the most able people. If you fail to do so, why would people want to come and work with you? Why would your customers, your clients and your stakeholders want to engage with an organization that is still rigid, over-ordered and over-hierarchical, rather than engaging with passionate people who understand what they're doing and know how to do it?

Diversity is strength

One area where the Department of Business Innovation and Skills has made significant progress is in increasing the diversity of its management and leadership team, where more than half of the top 140 managers are women. 'This gives us a range of role models,' says Martin Donnelly, and it has also encouraged a more collaborative approach:

I am regularly in meetings where there are one or two men and five, six or seven women. That is normal in BIS. We do not notice. Other people come here and notice because they think it's all about some quota. It's not about a quota at all. It's about empowering an organization that encourages diversity for everyone, and then you find you get a lot of very good women because they want to come and work here.

Generic principles of effective leadership

Although context is important, with smaller enterprises differing significantly when compared to a corporation or a large public sector organization, Martin Donnelly has found that effective leadership has some generic principles:

> You must lead from the top. You must have behaviours in your senior team and yourself as chief executive or permanent secretary or whatever that show that this is what you mean. You cannot have two sets of rules. You cannot say, 'One person behaves in this rather indulgent, individual way while some of his or her behaviours towards other people are under strain and aren't acceptable, but look at the number of things they've delivered.' There is no trade-off. People who do not want to work [collaboratively] in this way cannot have a place in the organization and everyone needs to understand that. We have values of supporting each other's successes, focusing on what matters most and empowering people to deliver.

For leaders, their contribution across the entire organization, not just in one department, must be encouraged. Part of the necessary cultural change means encouraging the whole person to be engaged at work. The Department has done work on the dominant narratives in the organization to deepen people's understanding of their role, and has hired the Royal Academy of Dramatic Arts to assist [their] leaders' ability to communicate:

People come back from that [training] with more confidence. [They have learned] some techniques that can be used to get better at connecting with their colleagues and listening to them. So as well as wanting to do it, you have to help people practise and learn how they can engage better in a non-hierarchical way. Making the case for non-conventional investments such as these, and for creating the space for improved leadership generally, requires the confidence to overcome the view that it is a bit of an indulgence.

If we don't do this, we can't meet the new challenges. There won't be more resource. We can't go on doing it this way. We can't expect people to work even harder. So how are we going to help ourselves to step back and respond in a different way to these new challenges? If we carry on in this way [Level 3], [then] sooner or later the private sector won't make any profit and in the public sector people will say, 'Oh, we'll just do it without you, or around you, or differently.' I think you have to say to people, 'There isn't a choice here. We must move in this direction.'

He also embraces the concept of *servant leadership*, or as one chief executive of an FTSE 100 company put it to him, 'I think of it as an upended triangle. The only justification for our existence is to make life easier for those people who are doing the work, rather than them supposed to be helping us.' He added, 'The *servant leader* brings his or her full personality and range of abilities into play, and ditches any idea of omniscience.'

Changing the mindset is critical, but one must understand also that, as a leader, you bring to the *management shift* your own inadequacies, weaknesses and vulnerabilities. Your humanity, if you like. Not your perfection, nor your overachievement, nor your obsession with getting every detail right. That's not the *management shift*. The *management shift* is saying, 'We do it because we're imperfect. We are people like each other who respect our differences and where other people are coming from, and we respect their home lives and their family lives because that's part of what they bring to work.' Therefore it only works if you treat people as fully rounded individuals, recognizing that obsession is the opposite to the *Management Shift* and that you need to work flexibly with people.

Innovasjon Norway – Norway

Norway, with its vast oil reserves and small population, benefits from possessing one of the world's largest sovereign wealth funds. It has a generous welfare state, though sharp falls in the price of oil in the period 2012 to 2015 did cause some economic problems. The publicly owned organization, Innovasjon Norway, was formed in 2004 with the goal of encouraging investment and industrial development. Anita Krohn Traaseth, Chief Executive of Innovasjon Norway, is overseeing a cultural change from a traditional bureaucratic set-up to one based on entrepreneurship. She used the *Management Shift* to improve engagement, declaring that, 'I've done it [the *Management Shift*] and it works. I mean, you have to figure out the context of your company, but the key philosophy here works.'

New mindsets, new culture

Creating an entrepreneurial culture cannot emerge from a simple reorganization. Much of the required change has to be at the individual level, it pertains to mindset and philosophy:

First of all, the way you described [in your book, *The Management Shift*] the different levels from 1 to 5 was helpful. I think they're really descriptive. Secondly, I think the three key words you identified in the book, engage, involve and exceed, really describes what this is about because you can't exceed if you don't engage, nor can you involve if you don't engage. Employee engagement is underestimated in many change processes. So I think those three key words are important. Thirdly, you're not just describing an organizational motive and a *shift*, [you are] also [describing] the importance of the *individual shift*. This is key, since organizations are made up of individuals. Change has to come from within and it begins with the individual.

In an organization with a bureaucratic heritage the change in culture and can be slow. Some of the key concepts and terms needed to explain the *shift* are not only radically different, they may provoke opposition, even ridicule:

When you work for the government and you work toward making industry and businesses more innovative, there is a fundamental passion for the task. However, the problems you face in the public [sector] when going from Level 3 to Level 4 are also about words. The semantics in Level 4 and 5 – enthusiasm, leadership, unlimited – are words that do not belong in an old, conservative, publically-owned culture and they will be ridiculed. There will also be a huge number of people who understand it and are longing for [more] focus on these simple words. [However], as long as you have a solid plan and a mission to support what you're trying to achieve, people will stick by it and prove it by delivering results over time.

Some of the resistance to the *shift* towards a more participative way of working is based on suspicion and/or prior conditioning whereby junior staff expect to be told what to do. Anita said:

They're used to getting answers from management, but when you involve them and say, 'So this is how we're thinking. What do you think?' they are like, 'What do I think? Aren't you supposed to come with the answer?' That takes time. They also become suspicious and say, 'Well are you asking us this because you want our input or do you have the answer already? We think you have the answer.'

Hence the importance of setting a direction and creating a vision. These responsibilities cannot be avoided. The participative part means people must be involved. This ensures that innovative alternatives are developed in order to achieve common objectives. Trust and transparency are essential. Anita Krohn Traaseth is as open with her staff about how much she earns as she is with the organization's goals. She facilitates monthly staff meetings that involve all of her staff; she also holds one-to-one meetings throughout the organization. It is unlikely that everyone in an organization will suddenly be enthused to move to a Level 4 culture, but at the outset a critical mass of engaged individuals will suffice:

> Every step counts and we're accountable for the progress, and then [you have to] repeat the drivers for change. That can never be over-communicated. Why are we doing this? What are the goals? How will we do it? What does it take from each and everybody? Then we report on progress. Have we reached it, what have we learnt from it and what is the next step? That's an effective and honest way to move from the old culture into a new one.

The goals are neither lofty nor vague, they are defined by the customer. Leaders often act as facilitators or advocates for the customer, especially in the early stages of a *shift* to Level 4. Then the conversations become focused around tasks, not special interests:

> We are here to make sure that the company is relevant for the future, where the customers define relevance. That's not the Workforce Council and that's not the management. It has to be the market and the customers who decide relevance, and we have to adapt and find a way to do that.

Openness and trust create engagement

The Level 3 way of implementing a programme of change is for an elite cadre to decide the new direction, then the organizational structure rolls out a programme of change using memos and instructions. In the short term this might appear to be more efficient because fewer people are involved and consulted, but it can lead to a false economy when people within the organization have insufficient knowledge of or commitment to the new vision. Steps often have to be retaken, morale may fall and talented people leave. Yet, when you take people with you, you win over hearts and minds in a Level 4 way. Initially it is slower, but, typically, you only have to do things once. Anita Krohn Traaseth explains:

> So I think when you are moving an organization from Level 3 to Level 4 you cannot decide that it's going to be successful. You have to learn by doing it and by taking it step by step. You have to engage not only the employees, you have to engage the whole ecosystem – meaning the Workforce Council and the board – and we get lots of tasks from the ministries, four different ministries. When you work on a transparent milestone plan, the best way is to communicate and share.

Change often meets resistance. This is sometimes rational, sometimes to protect vested interests and sometimes out of fear. However, she finds that the healthiest response is honesty and transparency:

> When people try to stop the process and go after you as a person, the only way to protect yourself is to be open and transparent and share experiences at every step. Because our company is owned by the Norwegian people, every Norwegian can send a letter to my company and ask for information because we [comply with] the law of publicity. For example, I put my hiring contract on a blog so everyone can see my contract. What is my salary? What are the terms that I'm hired on? I'm all for openness and transparency. In any transition the leadership has to take the first step [toward openness] and if you don't do it you won't get the trust that you need. You have to be open and you have to be honest and you have to learn from your experiences and you have to share that learning with the organization.

With this approach, she successfully persuaded the unions to become involved with the change programme even though the change resulted in some posts being lost, mostly managerial ones, as the organization became slimmer and more responsive. 'You cannot organize the changes yourself, you have to change people's behaviours because they are so used to working in a silo.'

Technological challenge

As noted in Chapter 1 (sub-heading Productivity), organizations must continually modernize their technology, but equally important is that they must ensure that the best use is made of this technology. This cannot be done unless people are managed well. 'You cannot digitalize work processes if they don't work. You have to fix them first.' (See also Chapter 1 on productivity). She added:

> We have had under-investment in technology over the past ten years, so digitalizing our services was extremely important, [but] you have to look at the culture, the work processes and the needs of the customer first – then digitalize. When you digitalize you do it stepwise, otherwise projects that are too big and too expensive will fail.

Outcomes

A more empowered workforce with an entrepreneurial Level 4 culture has now started to impact at Innovasjon Norway:

> The organization has never delivered such great operational results in such a demanding change process. In 2015 we set a clear goal to reduce the feedback time to entrepreneurs who applied for start-up grants. When you're doing a transition from Level 3 to Level 4 you must never lose sight of the market and the external affair, so we decided to make seven promises to our customers, one of which was to reduce the time taken to process startup grants from sixty days to just four days. Several of our offices are

now reporting that they have achieved this, and this makes me extremely proud.

Attraction and retention of talented people, especially the younger generation, has also been boosted by the move toward Level 4 and Level 5 ways of working:

> We also need to talk about the hard things about the *shift* because this is not easy work. So why are we doing it? Because if we're not doing it, we're not doing our job. We're not taking the company to the next level where it will secure its future. We will lose our top talent because they don't want to work for companies who stay at Levels 1 or 2. So if you're going to attract the next generation workforce, you have to be Level 4 or Level 5.

Reflections

At the heart of empowering leadership there is a paradox; to gain control you have to cede some control. The Level 3 mindset, that everything can be monitored, directed and overseen, is counter-productive. It can work for a straightforward task that you are doing yourself, but not for leading a complex organization. Anita Krohn Traaseth concluded:

> This is also a continuous process. It's not something you do once and then you're done. It has to be part of your culture. You have to accept that you cannot control everything. You have to let go of the traditional management skills and develop new ones and no one is born to do this. You have to learn this.

City of Glasgow College – UK

The City of Glasgow College was created in 2010 by the merger of three colleges: the Central College Glasgow, the Glasgow Metropolitan College and the Glasgow College of Nautical Studies.

From a necessary merger to transformed leadership

When these colleges were merged to form the new City of Glasgow College the institute's leaders decided to use this period of change to usher in a cultural change by modernizing the leadership and transforming the approach of the college from a command and control style to a more coaching, empowering model. As Paul Little, founding Principal and Chief Executive of the College, described in an interview for this book, 'We moved away from the *sage in the stage,* as you will, to the *coach in the side* and we're very much into fostering an enablement culture.' This approach was formed, in part, by his experience at Harvard University where he says, 'I probably learned more from the course participants than I did from the professors, but in many ways Harvard set that up to allow me to do that.' To make such a transition effective, it is necessary to view culture and values as being central. He explained:

> Values have played a huge role in that because we kept it down to six simple values, six straightforward values. The first one was the individual. We also included excellence, inclusion, honesty, integrity, and quality and diversity. The challenge was to try and establish those values as the bedrock of the college because we've always believed, and I've always believed as a change leader, that culture is at the heart of what we're trying to do. Formerly, maybe, we had a militaristic command and control type culture in an academic setting.

Central to the new approach is the Level 4 mindset of leadership and innovation, which is a marked departure from a Level 3 approach that is rooted in the impulse to control everything. The difference is more than just a different set of skills or competencies, it is a different mindset and a different philosophy. As Paul Little said, 'it means acknowledging uncertainty and accepting that you can lead change but you cannot manage change.' He added:

I don't think success is inevitable and certainly we usually try to inspire our managers by saying that their role is not to manage the inevitable. Their role is, as I mentioned earlier, to create the impossible and achieve the improbable.

Not replacing the classroom: evolutionary change

The change means embracing new challenges but not changing everything, given that the existing colleges had considerable strengths:

> I think my generation may have been looking for learning and occupations and careers, perhaps even status and, maybe, even a degree of fulfilment. I think the education leaders of the future will have to deal with a much more disparate galaxy of learners who can't be mass educated, who want their education done in shorter time spans, who want to make greater use of technology, who want to be inspired and who want to be co-creators of their own learning.
>
> We think that change happens at least four times faster outside the classroom than inside. With that kind of awareness, we are at least trying to embrace a leadership that prepares for ambiguity and uncertainty, while preparing for demanding learners. In this building every single space, even where we're being interviewed, is a learning space. You could even argue my office is a learning space. We think learning will become maybe more informal in the future and that peer learning and social learning will become more important as students learn from each other.
>
> With this approach educators see themselves as being inspirers rather than lecturers, with the result that the teaching staff become more open and communicative. They embrace social media and see communication with students as being continual, not reserved for the formal classroom sessions. [You need to be] more inclusive. You're communicating in real time, but you are also listening and reflecting on [what you hear].

Nonetheless, Paul has found that it is important to retain the essential disciplines of traditional education. Online learning can democratize the student experience, but 'I don't see it ever replacing the classroom on a mass scale. You can never replace the fundamental relationship between the inspirational teacher and the student in the classroom.'

Mergers often hit problems because elements of culture and values are downplayed. The leadership team at Glasgow College made a conscious decision to prioritize an empowering culture throughout the merger process, rather than treat it as an afterthought to the structural change:

> The conscious move to a Level 4 culture was concurrent with the move from eleven old campuses to two modern ones. The challenge is that you can, superficially, and in terms of systems and maybe even structures, achieve that [change], but to win over hearts and minds [can] take up to ten years. The advantage that we have is that we've reduced the number of sites we had from eleven to two. I think that on an emotional level people can move out of old surroundings and into new surroundings. Because of our constant communication, our constant consultation and our constant feeling of inclusion, we were able to keep the staff fully on board.

The college employed a psychologist to advise on the formation of affinity groups and their composition that, 'Allowed us to restructure on a human scale.' Around one in ten of the staff were involved with implementation groups. This formed a representative number without overly disrupting the teaching. He added:

> It was important that [both] the leadership team and I bore in mind that people have real, human connectivity and that we had to be empathetic to that. We had to be mindful of that in both the decision-making and in the creation of the systems, structures and plans that we put in place.

Constancy of purpose

The leadership at Glasgow College made it clear that they were determined to modernize both the organizational and the teaching ethos. They would make a success of the merger. To bolster a sense of security, staff were given a three-year guarantee that no one would lose their job in that period. Research for *The Management Shift* and elsewhere confirmed that purpose and a clear sense of direction, encompassing social and personal enhancement as well as financial returns, is essential for the highest levels of engagement and performance at Levels 4 and 5. Paul Little said:

> This is very much a kind of paradigm shift in our understanding of the practice of leadership, because we are now in a new century with new challenges and those challenges are increasingly rapid and increasingly complex. I think, for us, the important thing is that we inspire the curious mind. We inspire enquiry. The blueprint for change is such that it's not just known, it is understood by the leaders and by the people being led.

He refers to nurturing a *reservoir of innovation* throughout the college, so that new ideas are not just the responsibility of an elite cadre at the top of the organization.

The role of The Management Shift

Leaders at Glasgow College formally implemented the *Management Shift* in order to facilitate the required changes:

> I believe that if no one is following you, you're not a leader. [If] you're really going to walk ahead of people, you have to bring people with you on the journey. Making a *shift* to the next level requires guiding, coaching and mentoring, so we're obviously delighted to have the [*Management Shift*] programme. It gives us a very structured vehicle to achieve [our objectives]

as we try to ensure that we retain and develop our talent by using succession and talent strategies.

Leadership is very context-specific, and cannot be fully understood in terms of generic competencies, he finds:

We try and ensure that we match the appropriate leadership style to the appropriate leadership challenge and, obviously, we hope that the *management shift* will allow staff to reflect a bit more about that and be a bit more purposeful. Also, in learning to be a coach and being coached, we hope that they will use these skills within their respective teams. We're mindful that, very often, leadership is quite situational so the [*Management Shift*] tools and techniques and philosophies resonate strongly and loudly with us.

What has been the effect on morale, the ways of working and the culture? He referred to greater cohesiveness and inter-dependence within the team:

I've also seen the development of stronger, more trusting relationships. I have been impressed by [my] colleagues [in their] ability to give constructive feedback in a way that has an impact, in a way that doesn't destroy and in a way that encourages or, dare I say it, even inspires? I have seen some of the coaching partnerships where alliances developed between areas that I didn't think would develop. Individuals found shared interests and shared reliance. Sometimes I'm sure some of the staff would say, 'Well what about the City of Glasgow College way?' The *management shift* for us will be the City of Glasgow College *shift*, albeit the *shift* is for our institution in our setting and for our mission and for the people we serve.

What the methodical approach of *The Management Shift* has done for the City of Glasgow College has been to break down the difficult challenges of culture, engagement and performance into identifiable steps. He found that:

When you analyse the step change transition you find that they're just a whole series of incremental changes that are close together. Breakthroughs are rather rare and even the best breakthroughs require a huge amount of determination, purposeful inquiry, and trial and error for many years prior to that.

Results

Despite enduring one of the deepest recessions in modern times, the College's leaders managed to secure £200 million of funding from the private sector to help build the modern facilities. The motto of the college is, 'Let Learning Flourish'. The successful merger and culture change programme, supported by the *Management Shift*, enabled this sense of purpose to be embedded. Paul Little said:

> For me, the benefit is that more learners flourish more often, more dreams are fulfilled more often, more staff are feeling more fulfilled more often, and that we now have more leaders and they're better leaders than we had in the past. This year, for the fifth year in a row, our success rates have increased.

50 key strategies for the *shift* in public sector

Every situation is unique, with each management and leadership approach having to conform to its context. Sometimes, the systems and processes are strong but engagement levels are low. At other times, enthusiasm could be high but the processes not fully formed. In my research, I have found that the 50 Key Strategies (as set out in Table 2.1) are helpful when attempting to achieve the *Management Shift* in the public sector, but the precise mix still depends upon the context. Hence, it is necessary to read the case studies and to understand

TABLE 2.1 50 Key strategies for the shift in public sector

STRATEGY	CULTURE	RELATIONSHIPS	INDIVIDUALS	STRATEGY	SYSTEMS	RESOURCES
1. Leaders must show vulnerability and humility, not perfection	√		√			
2. Communicate a consistent, clear message			√	√		
3. Have a clear vision, one that can be adjusted on the journey. Repeat this continuously	√		√	√		
4. Stick to the key values	√					
5. Culture is at the heart of everything	√					
6. Have a blank sheet mentality, question everything	√		√			
7. Foster innovation and ideas	√				√	
8. Establish coaching and mentoring processes	√				√	
9. Understand the importance of the language used (TMS levels)			√			
10. Match leadership style to leadership challenges			√			
11. Repeat drivers of change			√	√		
12. Implement incremental changes				√	√	

(*Continued*)

TABLE 2.1 (*Continued*)

STRATEGY	CULTURE	RELATIONSHIPS	INDIVIDUALS	STRATEGY	SYSTEMS	RESOURCES
13. Use a trial and error approach	√			√	√	
14. Use a purposeful enquiry approach	√				√	
15. Have critical mass for the shift	√		√			
16. Build trust	√	√	√		√	
17. Use academic theory within the context of the organization					√	
18. Learn by doing					√	
19. Engage the entire ecosystem in the *shift*		√		√	√	
20. Ensure openness and transparency	√					
21. In the public sector, a leader creates a formula for the *shift*, and then implements it			√			
22. *Speed date* with employees to elicit their views		√	√		√	
23. Use *Time Thief* analysis to elicit unnecessary bureaucratic processes				√	√	
24. Collect feedback on what is not working					√	
25. Provide leadership and decisions			√			

26. Change the organizational design to remove silos	√	√			
27. Reduce the number of middle managers		√			
28. Empower people to make their own local decisions and deliver					√
29. Do competence mapping	√				
30. Use reflection instead of evaluation			√		√
31. Understand the role of technology and how it changes the way of working		√	√		
32. Ensure that top management have technological expertise		√	√		√
33. Let go of control			√		√
34. Use collaborative teamwork			√	√	√
35. Only reward behaviour that is consistent with the *shift*		√			√
36. Lead from the top			√		
37. Lead across the organization		√	√		√

(Continued)

TABLE 2.1 (Continued)

STRATEGY	CULTURE	RELATIONSHIPS	INDIVIDUALS	STRATEGY	SYSTEMS	RESOURCES
38. Choose values that support a focus on people	√		√	√		
39. Focus on what matters most			√	√		
40. Do not tolerate old ways of working	√		√			
41. Understand the importance of training	√		√			
42. Use storytelling				√		
43. Move from being a leader and act as figurehead to real people			√			
44. Help employees to engage in a non-hierarchical way	√		√			
45. Focus on shared purpose	√		√	√		
46. Work flexibly with people, depending on their life circumstances	√			√		
47. Understand the importance of gender balance	√			√		
48. Use the wisdom of the crowd and self-organization	√			√		
49. Move away from short-term agenda			√	√		
50. Understand that it is all about people	√		√			

one's own situation in as much depth as possible, as well as having an understanding of what the key strategies entail.

For each strategy, I have indicated the area of the 6 Box Leadership Model[3] to which that particular strategy is related (see Figure 2.1) This model has been chosen as a point of reference for the strategies presented in this chapter and in chapters, 3, 4 and 5 due to its extensive research and practical applicability, as described in *The Management Shift*[4] book.

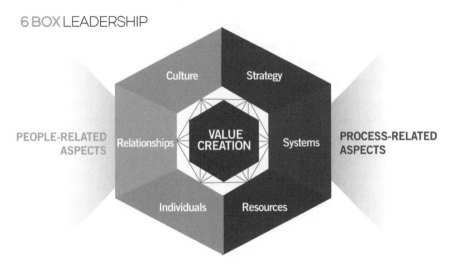

FIGURE 2.1 *The 6 Box Leadership Model.*

Source: Vlatka Hlupic: *The Management Shift – How to Harness the Power of People and Transform Your Organisation for Sustainable Success*, Palgrave Macmillan, October 2014

SEVEN REFLECTION POINTS FROM THIS CHAPTER

1 Have you learned to embrace paradox and ambiguity? Do you recognize that as a leader of a complex organization you sometimes have to cede control in order to gain control?

2 Do you pay equal attention to mindsets and individual *shifts*, as you do to new organizational set-ups?

3 Do you remember to inform and engage all relevant constituencies, including junior staff, the board, the owners and fellow managers?

4 How honest and open are you in your communications? Do you treat this as being at the heart of your leadership role rather than an occasional activity?

5 Do you identify and nurture a group of like-minded people who will help you effect change?

6 Do you let the customer define the problems to be solved and the tasks to be completed?

7 For difficult, *wicked* problems, do you put together diverse teams comprised of people who understand these difficulties best? Do you empower them to think of unconventional approaches?

3

Profit and principle combined: Inspirational stories from the private sector

KEY INSIGHTS FROM THIS CHAPTER

- If the leadership has a strong sense of purpose it is possible to secure better returns for shareholders while rewarding employees well.
- The best employers have observed these enlightened principles for decades and have demonstrated impressive resilience.
- It helps to move from a static Level 3 way of operating to dynamic Level 4/5 mindsets and behaviours.
- Technological and demographic changes may mean that the rigid hierarchies of Level 3 are no longer an option. Competitive organizations need to stay innovative, nimble and highly engaged in order to adapt to new contexts.

It's not a choice: the most enlightened employers return more to shareholders

In the previous chapter I noted how the phenomenon of increased public sector investment in technology and automation can lead to reduced productivity and waste. If you don't secure the engagement of staff and establish the right kind of leadership service improvements are unlikely to follow, irrespective of the scale of the investment. This is clearer still when using the 6 Box Leadership Model. The failed initiatives referred to were sometimes strong on strategy and resources, but weak on both processes and the three people-related dimensions. Alternatively, they were strong on the process side, but neglected culture, relationships and individuals altogether.

In moving from Level 3 ways thinking to the higher levels, one must reject the concept that different constituencies must be in conflict, i.e. the idea that if one person is winning then someone must be losing. That is not necessarily the case. With highly empowered, well- directed teams of people engaged with a strong sense of purpose, all stakeholders win. The sharp difference in mindsets can be summarized as shown in Table 3.1.

TABLE 3.1 *Examples of the differences between a Level 3 and a Level 4/5 mindset*

Level 3 Mindset
People are one of the company's resources. Managers need to secure the maximum productivity from them at the lowest cost that the market will allow for optimal performance.
Level 4/5 Mindset
People comprise the unique asset that creates all value. Research shows that if we harness their skills and engage them with a strong sense of purpose we will maximize the rewards for everyone with a stake in the business, including shareholders.

This chapter features exclusive interviews with senior leaders of corporations that have a long-term, principled commitment to the mindsets and practices of Level 4/5. In some cases they have held this view for many decades and have witnessed many Level 3 organizations come and go in that time.

Winning strategies from private sector organisations

Morning Star – USA

Morning Star, a transportation and food-processing company, was founded by entrepreneur Chris Rufer in California. It began production operations in 1990 and has grown rapidly since. Its democratic, open structure has been part of their culture from the very beginning. Doug Kirkpatrick, the original financial controller at the firm, attributed the company's success to this philosophy and to the engagement and innovation that it encouraged. Morning Star has grown from zero revenues in 1990 to become the largest tomato processor in the world with over $700 million in sales. It employs more than 3,000 people, including seasonal colleagues, but, prior to that, Chris' first working experience was very different:

> We had a number of managers and management layers. Below the management layer we had a layer of supervisors who directed the production activities and below the supervisors we had a number of coordinators and then at the bottom of the pyramid we had the people who did the actual work. We always had the sense that things could be better. Part of the insight came from the fact that every time there was an issue or a problem, or a conflict, dispute or question, that issue immediately went to the top of the pyramid on Chris' desk. We were getting virtually zero value out of the organizational structure.

Chris left that company in the late 1980s to start a new tomato processing company, and that company was Morning Star.

The Morning Star Colleague Principles

We met in a little dusty construction trailer on the jobsite and he [Chris] passed around a document called the *Morning Star Colleague Principles*. Essentially, there were two principles: first was that people shouldn't use force against others, second was that people should keep the commitments they make to others. As we talked about these principles we realized that these principles make up the foundation of law everywhere in the world, and they're the most basic fundamental principles of human interaction.

We all kind of looked at each other and we saw no reason not to adopt these. That was the moment that our fledgling company adopted the principles of self-management, realizing, even before the concepts were fully articulated, that a shift from Level 3 to Level 4 would lead to a more successful company and would actually help employees. Chris always sought ways to improve every aspect of the enterprise and is genuinely committed to fundamental human principles.

We experienced our first kind of qualitative experience with self-management when we built the first factory in 1990. We felt that we could not have built the factory as quickly as we did or brought it successfully online as quickly as we did had we structured ourselves on a hierarchy of command and control official channels of communication.

Self-management through the entrepreneurial mindset: making the complex simple

Most start-ups have a strong team ethic and little hierarchy when they begin. The challenge is to maintain this [essence of minimalism] when the organization becomes larger and some structures and processes have to be introduced. Chris' company managed to retain this teamwork structure by establishing a system of accountability rather than hierarchy:

We were a tiny band of twenty-four colleagues operating out of a tiny farmhouse in Central California [when starting out]. We were already kind of self-managing because we were all working extremely long hours, we were probably working 100-hour weeks just trying to pull this project off. We didn't have time for a lot of formalities, things were just moving too fast. We simply accepted these principles and kept on going. The *management shift* was a formal recognition of the way we were already operating.

The factories are laid out so that they're kind of broken up into discrete areas of responsibilities, so a person working in steam generation was basically the CEO of that part of the factory. It wasn't really formalized or necessarily written down anywhere, but it was very clear.

The *shift* is massive and, as I look at my experience with the first company where I started versus Morning Star, it's an example of Level 3 versus Level 4 (or four and a half). It is the difference between being in a controlled environment where you know people are guarded and cautious – who you know are unwilling to be themselves at work and embrace change, opportunity, teamwork and prosperity – compared to what most of us experience at Morning Star. Without putting an exact price tag on it, I would say it's the difference between mere existence and true happiness.

Morning Star colleagues do not discuss work-life balance to a great extent, but there is a strong emphasis on belonging and purpose at work. Our colleagues have a personal mission, supported by scorecards that they use to measure their own productivity and performance. We want work and life to be one and the same. I cannot imagine why a start-up would not want to embrace the opportunities of self-management, and I would think that *tech*' companies would be natural for self-management.

[It is] a great opportunity to manage great complexity through great simplicity. I think [the] mindset [factor] is huge. People think they have control in a Level 3 environment, [but] they only have the illusion of control. You only have control when people are engaged around purpose and meaning, when you have trust and communication. You can unlock the innovation of an entire enterprise by giving people a voice and a stake in results.

Morning Star sees leadership as being relevant throughout the enterprise, it's not confined to the senior level. Colleagues are encouraged to step up to their responsibilities and to be held to account for their decisions and performance. By contrast, in a more bureaucratic, hierarchical organization there are more opportunities to shift blame on to others and to have decision making unnecessarily slowed down.

WL Gore – USA

Self-organizing, non-hierarchical teams

Another organization that has been run on the basis of self-managed teamwork for many years is the hi-tech fabrics manufacturer WL Gore, famous for Gore-Tex waterproof clothing. Bill Gore started the company in 1958 having left DuPont, which was a hierarchical company. He had, however, previously worked in a creative, high-performing team and he wanted to re-create that *buzz* throughout the entire organization of his new firm, not just for the select few. Kevin O'Brien, a former senior manager at the company, said:

The way you've changed the style of communication and the words that leaders use in these organizations [in *The Management Shift*] is so applicable, and I could immediately see my own experiences reflected in those types of leaderships. I've worked in an organization that was not like Gore. I can really use my own experiences to kind of pinpoint where I see different styles.

Two-way communication

When you're interacting with a leader [at WL Gore], your first conversation and almost all your [subsequent] conversations are much more two-way. Sometimes they are one-way, but when they are they are focused on your needs rather than the leader's needs. There's a lot of discussion about what you are interested in working on, what your skills are and what the business needs are.

The approach is very similar to Morning Star in that it is accountability rather than a formal place in the hierarchy that creates discipline and focus. Individuals are empowered to complete their objectives and are held responsible for delivering what they have committed themselves to. They have the authority to seek out whatever resources they need to fulfil their commitments. There is no micro-management about the *how*; people have a fair amount of autonomy on the method:

It's like a golden rule, you always fulfil your commitments. It's a focus on the business and customer needs. That's a long-term strategic project. There's a lot of direct one-on-one communications, which I find works out much better in terms of fulfilling needs because you get less miscommunication when people communicate directly. WL Gore is, in a way, a purpose-driven organization that has the high level mission to be a fluoropolymer product innovator. The company has been consistently profitable since 1958 and has never had a loss in its entire business lifespan of almost sixty years.

The benefits, I think, are threefold. Firstly, from an organizational and business perspective, operating at Level 4 is very hard to compete with. Secondly, you end up being a lot more responsive to customer needs. Finally, the benefits of being in an environment where you're cultivating your individual purpose, your personal commercial mission of sorts, is something that [helps] you find your highest contribution.

I feel that in trying to engineer outcomes we've stopped asking people what it is that they're really interested in and what they really enjoy working on. My advice is that you should spend some time thinking about your own purpose and, just to clarify, purpose is not defined by outcomes like money but in the work you that actually enjoy doing and are skilled at. At Level 4, living your purpose through the work you do is essential for everyone in the organization, especially for the work of the leaders.

Sanofi Pasteur – USA

Starting a social movement

'Dear Mr CEO, I think we could do something, because it would be good for the company and it would be good for the business. We could better connect with our customers if we were as diverse as they are.' With this simple letter, written by employee Celine Schillinger, the pharmaceutical company Sanofi Pasteur began a diversity journey that was accompanied by a move towards a sustained Level 4, highly-engaged way of working. 'So I set up a group on the internal social network,' says Celine:

> It took me fifteen minutes, and here we are. We started launching activities, lunch, debates, inviting guests, organizing polls, etc. We had no budget, but we were very creative. We had people from diverse and very different functions and very different levels. Diversity is not just a women's issue, it's a people issue because men also suffer from the stereotypes that drive the company in the way they select people. The aim was to broaden the definition of a leader.
>
> Within just a few months, the movement grew to 2,500 members. It became a powerful, visible force. The topic became visible. We created awareness and we created a movement. The movement empowered some people who were totally silent before, but who had now found a purpose. It created very strong links and bonds between people who didn't necessarily

hold things in common before, and this is now producing value. Every place I go, I have friends thanks to this network and we do things together, we co-create.

This movement has produced value for the company. On top of that, it has produced a lot of image value because our movement has won several prizes, including a national prize granted by the minister for women's rights. We've also created a *network of networks* – a community of diversity networks between large companies that exchange ideas on best practices. Every year, it organizes a big event in Lyon with between 250 and 300 attendees.

The company discovered that bringing people together around a shared purpose taps into huge reserves of energy, which generates multiple benefits for the business, the people employed, customers and the society within which it operates.

Mobilizing stakeholders

The next stage was wider stakeholder engagement:

Some people had told me, 'Yeah, your gender balance initiative is popular because it's a fashionable topic, it's a popular social issue.' I said, 'No, I think it works because that's the way people want to work now, both customers and employees. We want to be inspired instead of having stuff imposed upon us, we want to choose and decide and we want what we want. We don't want to be passive and just receive information from experts, whoever they might be.'

As a customer, you no longer sit on your couch simply receiving images from a television. When you activate your computer or smartphone you're actively making searches, you're making choices, you're responding, you're challenging brands and you're checking with other customers whether the company tells the truth, or not. You are challenging authority. That's the way things work now.

You can turn your employees into activists. If you can inspire, enable and empower them to be communicators on behalf of the company you can unlock a lot of positive energy. For example, it takes two to three weeks to issue *The Perfect Press Release*, which we then push to journalists and hope that they will not change a comma or word. I think it's so funny, because this binary method is an outdated way of working; it is not the world in which we are living. People now look for themselves, they check with their peers and they don't need a journalist to explain everything.

Creating a purpose based community: a collaborative fight against the disease

The stakeholder engagement vision led Celine Schillinger to nurture a purpose-based community, a community of activists to fight against a disease. Originally, the company recommended that the community be based around its soon-to-be-launched vaccine. However, Celine decided that it would be more engaging to organize around the purpose rather than the product. An entire community is involved in fighting the disease, which involves wider societal issues and has a broader sense of engagement:

> I suggested that we create this virtual meeting room so that people could connect and this connection would, hopefully, create new solutions. Our interest was to establish a very lively ecosystem against the disease and to be a part of that ecosystem. We wanted to become activists ourselves, to be at the same level as other people and to support them. It was also a fantastic way to garner goodwill from other big organizations that were also fighting disease. The end result was the creation a community that is unusual in the world of *pharma*, an alliance of partners that connects the scientific world to the lay public.

> In the first week, and without advertising, the community had 10,000 followers on Facebook. Within a couple of months this figure reached

100,000. After six to seven months, there were 250,000. This happened because we took a completely different dialogue approach, because now it's about co-creating with other people and it's about connecting activists and so on.

In 2014 the project received an award for the best use of social media for healthcare (the Shorty Awards). In 2015, it received the Most Impactful Emerging Initiative Award by one of the leading pharma conferences in the world. More awards came later. People started to understand that it's not by adding new procedures, new people, new controls and by doing more of the same that you change something, it's by radically changing the way we work and by inspiring people to want to do a fantastic job.

I've read *The Management Shift*. I'm extremely hungry for those kinds of readings. I was very interested to read the theoretical backing to all of that because, from where I come, it reinforced the things that I've felt and the things I've discovered, but here was a whole corpus of research. I think it should be a mandatory read for any analytical type of manager.

Finding new people, finding new voices, being viewed as an enabler gives insights, gives goodwill and it gives a competitive advantage. We been here since the beginning so if our competitors try to come in we already have this learning and we are higher in the learning curve as regards social media and how to interact with our stakeholders.

Human-centric focus seems to be lost sometimes

The business impact of changing how we work has been phenomenal. It is a very different, more open way of working compared to the insular Level 3 corporate way. It involves individuals opening up and sharing what matters to them, including their life aspirations and what they really care about, not just their immediate work-related tasks. It's about encouraging the sense that each individual can make an impact. I see too many people abdicating their power to think and act independently. What can I do?

Change starts with me. Fighting for gender balance was my way of answering the call for commitment, but it could have been something else really. My advice is, 'find like-minded people and do something.' My final comment would be, 'don't try to follow or mimic others.' Role models are not here to be imitated. They are here to inspire other people to grow beyond their own boundaries, and everyone has their own way. Try the following: discussion, talking to people, interacting, challenging your own ideas and beliefs, learning, sharing and being comfortable with diversity of thought. From then on every path is open.

HCL Technologies – India

HCL Technologies is one of the top five technology companies in the world. Vineet Nayar, a former CEO of the firm, introduced progressive measures that transformed the culture of the organization, moving it toward a high-engagement, high-performance way of operating. Key to making the decision was to understand that this involved radical changes in processes and behaviours, not just incremental steps. It resulted in the counter-intuitive slogan, 'Employee first, customer second':

> What is the core business of our company, a company that gives differentiated value for our customers? Who created this? It was our employees, therefore what should the business of managers and management be? Obviously the business of managers and management will be to enthuse and to enable the employees who create the value. Hence the slogan, 'Employee first, customer second' was born. That is how we moved from being a $700 million company to a $4 billion company today, with a market capitalization $1.4 billion. The value will only exist if your idea is of real importance and, when you're dealing with people, it is very important.

The three-step framework for implementing the *shift*, as articulated by the company, is follows:

1 Create significant dissatisfaction with the status quo.

2 Create a vision for tomorrow, a vision that is so compelling that everybody jumps from their bed and goes to work for that reason. [It] is not where the company will go but where *you* will go.

3 Ease of experimentation will then take us from here to there.

What matters to me is that more and more people were willing to say that they worked for HCL. Customers were intrigued by the fact that they came second and many of them didn't understand this argument. However, they have now experienced a new situation where the person in front of them made decisions on behalf of the company. These were motivated and energized people who were empowered to create value for the customer. So our customer satisfaction rate increased. Our share price also did well and because our motivation went up revenues went up, profitability went up and customer satisfaction went up.

HCL Technologies made counter-cyclical investments in the recession that followed the 2008 banking crash. They had made a commitment that they would create 10,000 jobs in the US and in Europe and further said that, because they worked so extensively in the US and Europe, they would be part of the solution not part of the problem.

Handelsbanken – Sweden

Anders Bouvin, a CEO of Handelsbanken UK, reflected on the beginnings of his bank. The bank was created in its present form in 1970. Like WL Gore, it has held to the principles of collaboration rather than relying on an excessive hierarchy. In the late 1960s the bank was focused on volume, i.e. the number of accounts, product sales and lending volumes. The bank was also experiencing problems, but the appointment of Jan Wallander proved to be a radical, inspired decision. He introduced a very different model, which has been fine-tuned and retained to this day.

Strive to do better than your peers, remove absolute goals and cut the costs

One of his first reforms was to reduce the number of targets. In those days there were a multiplicity of targets, so he removed all of those and introduced one single financial goal. This was to have a higher return in equity than the average of our competitors. It was all about doing better than one's peers rather than having an absolute set of goals. 'We haven't done a budget in Handelsbanken for over 40 years, we don't believe in fixed planning':

> In order to achieve this goal we needed to excel in two areas. One area was to have the highest level of customer satisfaction and the other area was to have lower operating costs than our peers. The three cornerstones of the bank are the goal itself together with the two means to reach that goal.

Empower people who are best suited to understand the needs of customers

Wallander's reforms were fundamental. He asked penetrating questions about the nature of customer service and customer satisfaction. This led to the question, 'Who in the organization is best suited to satisfy our customers' needs?' The answer to that was 'it was those who are closest to the customer!' If you want treat the customer better, you have to empower the people who deal with them. Anders Bouvin added:

> Wallander flattened the pyramid and got rid of layers and layers of middle management, people who really didn't add value for the customers and whose roles were no more than to tell other people what to do and then follow up [to ensure] that they did as instructed.

[By doing this] we not only reduced our costs and complied with the core means to reach the goal of having lower costs than our peers, we also introduced a system whereby customers were serviced locally by local people who were empowered to make decisions. We call it the *church spire principle*: 'Banking shouldn't be conducted over a larger geographical area than you can actually see if you crawl up the local church tower.'

This concept is really about the local community base and being close to your customer. If you actively encourage people to take responsibility, those people will not run off and take silly decisions. Instead, they will become even more prudent and even more careful when it comes to ensuring that the correct decisions are made.

The purpose of the Handelsbanken head office is to support the branches. It doesn't instruct the branches on what to do. Discipline is maintained by a strong corporate culture that has binding principles and values, and these are known and shared by everyone who works there:

It's about trust and respect, and getting the best out of people. If you encourage people to take decisions, they will take that step forward and the quality of the decisions taken, the thousands of decisions taken every day, will be of a much higher quality than you can ever have in a traditional command and control structure.

Since the bank introduced this way of working, it has enjoyed a higher return on equity every year for over forty years, and it has consistently scored highly in independent customer satisfaction surveys. Handelsbanken even went through the international banking crisis of 2007 to 2008 without needing support from stakeholders or the state. It had previously survived an earlier financial crisis that affected Scandinavia in the 1990s.

Moving away from the bonus culture towards profit share model

Handelsbanken does not pay bonuses, which is consistent with its approach of avoiding sales targets and short-term goals. There is a strong emphasis on recruiting the best people and the pay is competitive. There is also a profit-sharing system which was introduced in the early 1970s called Oktogonen. The way it works is that a part of the profit accrued above the average return on equity for the industry goes back to the staff in the form of a foundation. That profit is then divided by the number of employees, which is then converted into a fund that invests mainly in Handelsbanken shares. You cannot withdraw your share of profits until you reach the age of sixty, even if you leave the bank. The profit-sharing scheme encourages long-term objectives and a focus on customer satisfaction. It also fosters cooperation. 'I think the key is to get all incumbents to break away from short-termism and short-term targets,' says Anders Bouvin. 'And I think that quarterly targets obstruct efforts to change, because you're stuck in this cycle, this short-term cycle.'

Johnson & Johnson – USA

Taking leadership training to the shop floor

The consumer goods giant, Johnson & Johnson, has had a corporate leadership programme, called Standards of Leadership for over twenty years. The company was decentralized globally, but did little cross-boundary working with other companies. When Mick Yates started as Company Group Chair, Consumer for Asia-Pacific, his goal was to take the programme to shop floor level. He recalled:

> We trained everyone on the same standards of leadership. It was at the beginning of the internet when people were just starting to use electronic means of communication. We actually measured the organizational change over a period of time (three years) and recorded how we were improving

against our various goals. We had seven questions, one for each of the standards and the last question was, 'Are we having fun?'

When I last saw him about eighteen months ago, Marshall Goldsmith told me that he still quotes the results we got. We got more employee engagement and we had more people interested in what we were doing. We certainly had a broader understanding among all of our people about what our strategies and priorities were and, eventually, we managed to get our countries working together in a better way.

Distributing decision making

When we first started this process, a young brand manager in Thailand asked me how things would change. I said:

Well today, if you have a problem you will talk to your boss and if your boss can solve the problem for you then fair enough. However, if your boss can't solve the problem they will talk to their boss, and if their boss can't solve the problem they will then talk to their boss and, eventually, it will get to the country manager. If they can't solve the problem, they will talk to one of our vice presidents and if they can't solve the problem it will end up on my desk. Of course I refuse to leave the problem unsolved, so I will <u>tell</u> you what the answer is. [Very command and control.]

In the new world, what will happen is this: you might have a problem and you may know somebody in Australia, perhaps someone who is not even in your department, but who may be able to point you in the direction of a solution. Even if they can't find a solution themselves, they may know somebody else who might be able to help and together they will come up with a couple of options. You'll then go to your boss and say, 'Here's my problem, here are my options, what do you think?' So in that way you, the brand manager, will actually be much more responsible for the leadership of your business.

Impact on the business

Every six months, senior managers would ask everyone in the organization whether they were more customer-focused, whether they were experiencing more collaboration and if they had sufficient space for innovation etc. They began to measure the results and all could see that, over time, most of those questions were supported by improving numbers.

Strategies for the shift

1 Firstly, the company made a clear statement as to what it was trying to achieve.

2 Secondly, managers made sure it was taken to the shop floor and wasn't just left with the top level managers.

3 Thirdly, the managers communicated regularly: in meetings, newsletters, town hall gatherings and question and answer sessions.

4 Finally, they carried out a lot of storytelling. Engaging stories that harnessed a sense of purpose and set out a realistic vision that people could almost touch and feel.

If employees are made to feel part of the system and are truly engaged, that will reduce workforce attrition. It will also make your business more sustainable and it will reduce your training costs. That's a big part of sustainability. Too many people think sustainability is only about products, recycling and so on, but, frankly, it's also about your organization. How can you develop your people in such a way that they'll want to stay with you and grow, and then develop other people in the same way?

Unilever – UK/the Netherlands

Doing well by doing good

Unilever has been one of the world's largest consumer goods companies for many decades. In 2010, the new Chief Executive, Paul Polman, surprised the corporate world by announcing that he was ending quarterly reporting and other short-term financial targets, and that he was committing the company to sustainability. Paul said:

> The firm was *doing well by doing good*, but somehow we hadn't connected that as strongly to our business model as Lord Lever had done when he invented Lifebuoy and Sunlight Soap. He had set very clear missions and was clearly driven to addressing major societal issues of the time. The reason I like this company is because we are in 190 countries, touching about over 2.5 billion people every day. We are simply soap and soup. You cannot find a more transparent, a more honest way of making a living.
>
> The years 2007 to 2008 posed big questions as to what was going on in this world. I think a lot of people started to realize that companies needed to have more of a purpose and they needed to transform their economic system to make it work for more people. Overconsumption, environmental stress and climate change being among the problems. Frankly this left too many people behind and incurred [considerable] amounts of debt at both government and private level. I think the situation now is probably even more difficult than it was then. We haven't, frankly, addressed all these issues.

The old business model is not working anymore

Paul's approach is a radically different ideology, not just a different emphasis. He criticized the concept, popularized by the famous economist Milton Friedman, that profits are the sole aim of business:

> When stock markets keep going up and when you have a better lifestyle every day, when you have more things and you can buy more things, don't you ask yourself, How is this being done? or What, exactly, is going to happen in the world? It's very clear to me that the forces that were coming together at that time, and which are still coming together, have never been

seen before. They require a different role from business, a different response from politicians and a different role from civil society.

We have a world where too many people are excluded and where there are planetary boundary issues, such as climate change, food security, youth unemployment, poverty, etc. Business has a role to play in trying to solve that.

In most parts of the world business is sixty per cent of GDP, eighty per cent of the financial flow and ninety per cent of the job creation. These issues cannot be solved if business does not step forward and take up a role. We all know that businesses will not succeed if societies fail, and business cannot simply be a bystander in a system that gave it life in the first place.

He talks about the *permission to operate* that businesses have to earn. This discussion goes back to the question of why business exists – business exists to solve problems and to improve situations that would otherwise deteriorate.

The Unilever Sustainable Living Plan

Unilever's goals are defined in terms of societal and environmental impact, not just sales. Higher standards of sanitation and hygiene, for example, form one important objective:

We are not just selling soap. We are in the business of helping children reach the age of five and getting into hand washing. All that [is a key part of the plan]. [It involves] all of our brands operating with a deeper purpose to deliver positive impacts. Dove fights for women's self-esteem while Domestos attacks the issue of open defecation. Even our ice cream brand is looking at job creation and employment through our *Feet on the Street* merchandising programme – it is an ideal brand to do that. Other things include: sustainable sourcing, social compliance in the value chain, women's empowerment, fighting against corruption, fair payment of tax, etc.

Unilever has become more externally focused and defines its purpose in ways other than just revenues or growth:

I've always made it very clear that by focusing on the consumer, by making our brands purpose-driven and by making that our main reason for being, our shareholders will ultimately benefit. Where we have conflict, it is [with] short-term shareholders or speculators who come in and out of the stock to make short-term money. Short-termism is the world's biggest challenge. You cannot solve poverty, climate change or food security by myopically focusing on quarterly profits. The company has a strategy for growth [that] has to be sustainable – narrow short-term indicators such as quarterly profits or GDP are no longer the only guides.

We spent a year, more than a year, getting the *internal* company together [to prepare them for the *shift*] because it's very clear that if your own people aren't on board or don't feel comfortable, then you will not be able to achieve the results externally either.

The first year, year-and-a-half, was very much spent on thinking about what we wanted to do and measuring and tracking all of the products in our total value chain. 'What's the impact on water, on waste, on packaging, on CO_2 across our total value chain?' We mapped all of that so that we could see where we had the highest impact by brand, and then we asked ourselves, 'What actions should we put behind them to ensure a positive impact on society?'

This became the Unilever Sustainable Living Plan (USLP), which the company launched internally in the second year and, from there, launched it publically in the third year. Managers set fifty targets, which the company accounts for publicly. These include objectives such as: sustainable sourcing, reaching a billion people to improve their health and well-being, totally decoupling growth from environmental impact, reaching people with efforts to improve oral care and nutritional health challenges and building toilets. Managers began monitoring these objectives against actual performance. These clear targets are key; transparency drives the trust so absent in major parts of society and it is this trust then forms the basis for prosperity.

Key steps

You need to find the model that empowers people and you also need to establish a structure that works, but it's not that simple. Your strategy needs to be clear and it all starts with basic principles. You must have a clear strategy together with a structure that is able to execute that strategy, and you need the right people. The most difficult thing to do is to work within the company's culture and the values, which we continue to do. That work continues to evolve as our company evolves, as new people come in and as the world changes.

An important adjunct to this strategy is individual leadership and culture. The *Unilever Leadership Development Programme* provides training programmes on self-knowledge, discovering your own purpose and finding out who you really are – you cannot be a leader of others without knowing yourself first. That was the first wave of these courses. The second wave was about influencing others, while the third wave was about *purpose in action* – putting one's knowledge into action to promote Unilever's purpose. The journey to becoming a more sustainable company never stops. You might think you know your purpose and you might believe that you have reached Level 5, but tomorrow you might only be a Level 4. Just because expectations suddenly changed.

Ingraining values in company DNA

How do you instil values in a company? We spent a lot of time on our company values, communicating these ideals, celebrating, explaining, living these ideals and empowering people to be role models etc. If you focus only on share price and neglect people then your business will likely degrade in the long term. The question of a higher purpose is placed at the heart of business planning, strategy and operations. If you are not driven by a purpose, you don't have a long-term business model.

He noted that the average length of a publicly traded company in the US is now less than sixteen years and that the average tenure of a CEO is just four-and-a-half years. These are the symptoms of short-term business models built on flawed premises.

Barriers to shift

There are many challenges when moving towards a long-term, sustainable business model. Above all, accounting systems need to be reformed. The present standards and approaches don't value many external sources of value, which means that businesses transfer these costs to others. I have always said that as long as we value a dead tree more than a tree that's alive, we're in trouble.

The first barrier is short-term versus long-term. The second barrier is man versus nature, which is the defining value that I talked about and took into account. The third barrier, if you want to call it a barrier, is the economic system that we have, what I call *the few versus the many*.

We have the answers to most questions, but everything is reduced to how we, as individuals, want to behave. Do we put the interest of others first, do we think inter-generationally, do we apply the *golden rule* in our thinking? How do you drive people toward a higher degree of morality, to put themselves at the service of others while recognizing that it's actually to their benefit that others do well? That's seems to be a difficult concept that many people seem to have lost sight of. So how do we bring morality back to business? Smart people can circumvent laws, rules and regulations and we've seen enough examples of that, but how do you put the interest of the common good ahead of your own interest? How do you diminish the power of greed?

Creating young leaders of the future

Academic and business environments are still not adequately preparing leaders for the emerging world of high populations that place a strain on the environment, of technological inter-connection and of continual change.

It is a world full of paradox and unintended consequences. I think the future definition of leadership in truly Level 5 companies will be one where leaders proactively encourage others to make transformative changes that go beyond their own company. It has less to do with scale because a small company can do this, but how do you make transformative changes that go beyond your own company?' Addressing these challenges is essential and we are now close to the point where the cost of not acting exceeds the cost of acting.

Benefits

You can have a world where nobody has to live in poverty, a world where everyone has equal opportunities. This does not mean that everyone is equal, it means that everybody should have the opportunity to access education, food, some sort of employment and an opportunity to participate to their fullest potential – a world where there are fewer and fewer haves and more and more have-nots is not working. If we don't address these issues we will ultimately challenge our own existence. Nature will win. If man is extinct, we will become another of these many species that is on the brink of extinction. It will only take another 150 years before the world returns to its original shape. It will laugh at us, but we won't be there anymore.

How quickly can we galvanize people into seeing this and have them act upon it? For example, 800 million people go to bed hungry every night – 800 million – and they don't know if they'll wake up the next day. Yet we waste thirty to forty per cent of the food in the supply chain while diabetes type 2 and obesity continue to create one of the greatest pandemic challenges the world has ever seen. You might say that fewer people now go to bed hungry now compared to twenty or thirty years ago, but clearly the issue hasn't been addressed quickly enough.

I looked at that problem when I chaired the G20 Task Force for food security. The cost to solve the problem was estimated to be £80 billion, while we wasted more than £500 billion of food in the value chain. Thus, the cost of not acting is higher than the cost of acting, yet we can solve these burning issues over the next fifteen years if we choose to do so. Indeed we would all be better off and it would be, perhaps, the biggest plan we have for economic growth and job creation. Personal willpower will be needed. It is itself a renewable resource, that's why I always say, 'we need more leaders and trees.'

Salesforce – USA

Salesforce, one of the largest cloud computing firms in California, is an organization that was founded upon transparency of goals, shared purpose, an absence of micro-management and the minimization of bureaucracy. 'Let your people be free to make decisions on their own,' says Charlie Isaacs, senior manager at Salesforce:

> Guide them when they need guidance, but establish achievable goals early on and allow your people to accomplish what needs to be accomplished without too much scrutiny and questioning. It's almost like we don't even have an organization. We have an *org chart*, so you know who is responsible for everything. It's about who owns this and who then takes ownership of it.

Collect ideas from employees

When I was VP of Engineering at GTE (now part of Verizon), we built stuff. I would surprise the heck out of people when I went down to the factory floor and walked up to the lowest factory worker on the totem pole and said, 'Well, what do you think? Are things working the way they should be?' They replied, 'Well actually, no. I made this recommendation weeks ago that would improve our productivity and efficiency, but we never did it.' I said, 'Well, how does that make you feel when you're doing your work?' 'Well, it makes me feel frustrated, because we could do things a lot better, a lot faster, and higher quality.' So I said, 'Okay, we're going to make that happen.'

It was a large production line that was big enough to try new production processes. We tried her idea, but before we even attempted that she was *blown away* because she was a woman and I had listened to her. In fact, her idea revolutionized our manufacturing process, it saved us a lot of time and money and it improved efficiency. Morale within the company improved. People now knew that I was listening to them and I was acting upon their recommendations.

Salesforce has an internal social media platform called *Chatter* which is used by the firm's 18,000 employees. If anyone has an idea, they can post it on *Chatter* and seek offers of help with innovative ideas. The platform can also be used for surveys and questionnaires. It is a well-used innovative tool.

Aligning individual and organizational values

Purpose and values are articulated by the acronym V2MOM, which was a measure created by its founder, Marc Benioff. It stands for Visions, Values, Methods, Obstacles and Measures. In short, 'The vision helped us define what we wanted to do. The values established what was most important about the vision, it set out the principles and beliefs that guided it (in a specified protocol).'

How do you want to change the world and what do you want to do? What methods, obstacles and challenges are you going to meet in your attempt to create that vision? Do you need the organization to help you meet your goal? If so, how do we invest in that and how do we make that happen? Then measures, of course. Everyone in the organization has their own V2MOM, which is posted publicly. It is not just about own personal objectives, your V2MOM is a sub-set of your boss's V2MOM, which means that everybody in the company is aligned.

The method is the important part because that's the execution part. What are you going to do to get that job done? What are you doing to do to make that happen? We use Salesforce dashboards to show how you're doing, and you can pull in more data to substantiate your claims.

I'm the *IoT* guy at Salesforce, I do the *Internet of Things*. My goal is to make Salesforce the best platform for the *Internet of Things*, and that's my vision. Every customer who's a Salesforce customer, if they have a physical product or a service, should connect their product to Salesforce.

If he could, Marc Benioff would invite everybody – all 18,000 employees – to a meeting room, but that would be a cost-prohibitive. Instead, he brings together all the people that need to collaborate on a day-to-day basis and he then live-video feeds that management meeting to every employee. People are encouraged to contribute at the meetings and there is a *Chatter* feed running during the event.

Taking care of employees and giving back to the society

When someone asks me to make a presentation on innovation, I tell them, 'We attract innovative people because we attract nice people.' That's going to sound really corny, but we have this thing called the 1/1/1 Programme. [This] means that we give one per cent of our equity (Salesforce equity), one per cent of all of employees' time and one per cent of our product back to non-profit organizations such as NGOs. Employees get paid time off. Thus far, about $75 million has been handed to non-profits and the company has donated one million service hours.

Marc Benioff was named one of the 2015 highest rated CEOs by Glassdoor. Salesforce was named in the Fortune magazine as one of the most innovative companies for five successive years up to 2015. It's the fastest growing top-ten software company, having consistently grown by over thirty per cent year on year:

> Customers will come to you if they know you do the right thing and if you're a good company. If you exhibit the characteristics of Level 4, you'll grow, that is a by-product of performing Level 4 properly. Technology can also provide you with the resources to keep in touch with your customers better. The following questions should be at the top of management's priority list, 'How am I doing with my customers? How am I treating my customers? Do the customers like what I'm doing?'

Marc believes that employers who don't move from Level 3 to Level 4 are going to be threatened by companies that do. Not only does Level 4 increase adaptability and resilience, the culture also attracts the best talent. Exceptionally talented people don't want to work for Level 3 organizations, they want to work at Level 4 and Level 5.

Deutsche Bank New York – USA

Deutsche Bank, which is headquartered in Frankfurt, Germany, is one of the largest banking and financial services companies in the world. Its subsidiary, Deutsche Bank, New York has undergone significant changes in the past decade, adopting teamwork and high usage communications technology. In 2008, the bank was re-organized and the use of this collaboration technology increased. 'It was clear we were working like it's 1995,' recalls John Stepper, senior executive:

> It was as if the internet had passed us by. No searches, no self-publishing, no social media. Like many people I recognized that 'this was a great liberator,

a great equalizer.' Anybody can shape their reputation and build a network. All those ideas were out there. It was now a question of how do you help people apply them? How do you change their habits? Every day they're sitting in front of their inbox surrounded by people who just process emails and go to meetings.

Practice small steps with feedback and peer support

There followed a change in focus at the company with the introduction of peer support groups together with an innovation known as *Working Out Loud Circles*, which were all geared towards improving teamwork and communication:

The traditional mechanical model [of management] has limitations in dealing with complexity and tends to lead to slower decision making. It's poor at resource allocation, but it is good at certain things, e.g. certain kinds of optimization. Wal-Mart really did a fantastic job of reducing costs in their supply chain, you know, fantastic, but now when Uber comes along, what do we do? By the time you even are aware of it, you're done. So yes, while I think it isn't necessary for every organization the majority will shift towards Level 4 and 5. The only way to produce real sustainable change is with small steps practised over time, together with feedback and peer support.

When talking about the *shift*, author Frederic Laloux talks about the necessary, but not sufficient, conditions of having a CEO and a management board that believe in self-managing teams etc. 'If you have that maybe you have a better shot, but if you don't have it, don't bother. Maybe you could become a better Level 3.' I think that's what I would advise people as well.

Change may still be possible even without support from the most senior level, but it is unlikely to be transformational. Instead, individuals should look for more localized improvements in purpose, direction and performance.

Where possible, Stepper encourages people to undertake fast and cheap experiments to test what will work.

Working Out Loud

The concept of *Working Out Loud* is based on an understanding of the importance of relationships and communication. The best way to build relationships, particularly meaningful, authentic ones, is based on generosity. Humans are social animals and we are wired to reciprocate when people contribute to the network. Being visible is a central part of this approach:

> That's where the internet part comes in. You don't *have* to be visible, but [when you are] you amplify who you are and what you do. You expand the set of contributions you can make and how you can offer them. If *Working Out Loud* is about making your own luck, when you make your work visible you improve your odds even further.
>
> People often get stuck on the need for a specific destination or the one special purpose, but we focus on purposeful discovery. This helps you decide what kind of people you need to include in your network and which contributions ought to be made. Your goal could simply be a learning goal. A growth mindset means you understand that getting better at something is more about effort and practice than some innate ability.

What this approach does, he finds, is to tap into peoples' intrinsic motivators of autonomy, mastery, and purpose:

> They've got a little bit more control. It's not just about their boss, their performance rating and that kind of thing. They can build a network that makes them more resilient, that helps them access knowledge and makes them more effective. They can also increase their sense of relatedness to those people within their network, which then gives them a sense of purpose. That's great for the individuals.

What the firm gets are people who have formed a habit of working in a more open, generous, connected way that increases the digital literacy of the firm, while making tacit knowledge searchable and discoverable.

Working Out Loud is supplemented by other elements: different processes for HR, compensation, distribution and appointing people, but, wow, this is a lovely people-based, free, scalable movement. We deliver it by using self-organizing peer support groups called *Working Out Loud circles.*

The way we do it and the way other companies do it – the circles are in eleven countries right now – there's no centre, there's no management program and all of the resources are free. Sometimes we organize an event to explain what it is and then people sign up and self-organize. It doesn't matter what their title or rating is. No one checks on them, it's all confidential. It just spreads and what people say is, 'this made me feel better, this made my world bigger, this gave me a sense of hope or control and I feel more encouraged and connected to my colleagues.'

Horizontal changes versus a vertical shift

The approach places equal emphasis on the individual and the group. Each person is encouraged to believe that they can make a difference. If you can make work better for the people around you and if you're connected to social networks and other people around the world, you may not change the company and you may not be Level 4, but you could be a better Level 3.

That shift within a level makes it much more likely that you can go to the next level. You can send these ripples around your company, and it will be a very human change that helps individuals. The overall system might require some other ingredients, but what works and what's obvious in hindsight is that something must be done. It's more *Lean Start-up* than revolution. Do experiments. Find people like you. Do something. Get some more people. Do some more things.

Consequence of not shifting

The investment required to shift to Level 4 is considerable, but the risks of not shifting ought to compel organizations and managers to change. He argues:

> Large, hierarchical bureaucracies operating on the basis of the annual budget cycle and an annual performance review are likely to be too slow in their response to changing technology and demographics. Certainly in ten, twenty years from now we'll look back and think, 'What were they thinking? The planet is changing and they're doing the annual strategic planning off site!' It doesn't make any sense. For many, they just won't be able to deal with changes in the environment or with customers.

Barriers to shifting

Inertia can cause built-in torpor in some organizations. If you work at a big corporation and you made it to the top or the middle or wherever you are, you were always playing defence to keep that position as long as you could. That's barrier number one.

Barrier number two is everybody else suffering from *learned helplessness*. That is the way it is! Some just look up and say, 'Until someone else does something, there's nothing I can do'.

I can't do much about the first barrier, but I can do something about the second. I can empower people to genuinely make a difference, both for themselves personally as well as for their professional stature within the company.

The John Lewis Partnership, UK

Simon Fowler started the interview by explaining the origins of the John Lewis Partnership:

> The idea of the pioneer, John Spedan Lewis, who was the son of the founder of this UK-based department store, was simple. It was about how he could

run a business where employees in the business felt more engaged and held a greater interest in the business than the employees of its competitors. He started with profit-sharing and by creating an in-house magazine so he could share knowledge while ensuring that democratic principles were in place that allowed staff to have a voice in how the business was run. He understood the importance of engagement, internal communication, exchange of ideas and common purpose.

In 1929, one year after his father died, he signed the first trust settlement, the first legal step toward creating a form of co-ownership. John Lewis is now a trust-owned business, which means the terms of the trust, as embodied in the constitution, determine how the trust is executed.

When an individual becomes a permanent employee in the John Lewis Partnership, whether that is working for John Lewis, Waitrose or the Group, they become a partner. The governing authority resides in the chairman who holds all the decision-making rights and who can make any decision they want to make. However, the way the chairman uses that power is balanced by another governing body, the Partnership Council. Around the UK there are around eighty constituencies, each of which votes for a partner to represent them for a three-year term on the Partnership Council.

Seven principles

The first of these [seven] principles is the one that staff often talk about as being the ultimate purpose of the John Lewis Partnership, which is, 'The happiness of all its members through their worthwhile and satisfying employment in a successful business.' The remaining principles embrace power, profit, partners, customers, business relationships and community relationships.

Democracy at all levels

The business is an £11 billion undertaking that employs 85,500 partners in supermarkets, department stores, leisure facilities, farms, farm shops and the head office. Given its scale, there is a fair degree of decentralization with decisions taken locally on how best to improve the business unit, but this is balanced by the executive authority of the chairman and its senior managers.

Bringing humanity into commerce

I should probably just say that our aims are to bring humanity into commerce. My role is an independent board role. My purpose is to ensure that the constitution is fully complied with and that the voice of the partners is being heard by the board. It is not about shying away from the reality of commerce, it's about doing it in a different way, a way that gives us a better approach to doing business. You then gain a lot more engagement from people because they feel as if they have a lot more control over how things are being done, though not necessarily what is being done.

In this commercial landscape one often has to face the reality of things that are happening when you have no influence over them, but you do have an influence over *how* to deal with them. You might be fantastic at delivering job results, but your behaviour might be very poor and no matter how hard you try to move yourself up the pay and progression scale, you won't be able to succeed until your behaviour and your performance are both very good.

One of the beauties of the partnership is that we give partners a choice about the sorts of things they would like as a benefit. There are a number of benefits that the John Lewis Partnership offers. In addition to leisure facilities, other perks include six months paid leave after twenty-five years of service and a fifty per cent discount on food.

Engaging employees and customers for increased profit

Simon notes that Harvard Business School completed a study in 1997 after working with the Sears department store group. The research was summarized as *the employee-customer-profit-chain*. The researchers found that if you gain two per cent more engagement from your employees, you gain one per cent greater engagement from your customers and your profits increase by half of one per cent:

> In the John Lewis Partnership, there is a *partner-customer-profit-circle*. Partners share in the company's profits in the form of an annual bonus. Each year, the Partnership Board determines where the balance lies between reinvesting profits back into the business and returning profits to partners in the form of a bonus. This sharing of profits is expressed as a percentage of pay and it is balanced against the needs of the partners and the needs of the customers. By maintaining this balance we never get into an awkward circle where we're going after profit at all costs, to the extent that our business suddenly becomes very short-termist. Short-term knee-jerk decisions may increase profits initially, but they don't gain customer or partner engagement.

You can't value magic

> A lot of the value is in the magic. The magic that we're able to create because of our culture, because of our people and because of our collective passion. If you put a price tag on an organization like this you would always end up undervaluing it, and that seems to be a futile exercise when you have something so special. In most organizations it's the capital in the organization that employs people to get on and do the job, whereas here it is our people who employ the capital.

Herman Miller – USA

Values embedded in the company's DNA

Herman Miller's strong values were instilled by its founder, DJ De Pree. He was a deeply principled human being with strong values fuelled by his deep Christian faith. Those principles have been faithfully kept by his two sons,

Hugh and Max, who succeeded him as the business' leaders, and thereafter by subsequent CEOs. Current CEO Brian Walker says:

> The company has always believed that, ultimately, it would not be judged by its products and its profits, but by having a higher ambition which, I think, is always better for the DNA of a company. I think people who work here believe that the company stands for something unique and special.

Managing by principles where everybody is a leader

The company thrives on ideas rather than financial targets. If you can infuse the organization with the power of an idea you will accomplish much more than you could ever imagine. However, the company doesn't respond well to task or specific directives. Even the idea of a fairly significant transformation to the operating side of the company can cause concerns, such as when we installed the Toyota production system. At first folks rejected it because it felt like a series of activities, but once it was explained in a broader context people in the company began to see the vision. It was not about reducing costs anymore, it was about reducing human struggle. It was then accepted. Thus, by reducing human struggle we were able to manufacture products of a higher quality.

The other thing that sets Herman Miller apart, and we talk about this virtually every day, is that Herman Miller has been very much a company that manages more by principle than it does by policy. While we obviously need to have policies to run the business every day, we try to spend most of our time in areas where we're engaging with our employees or setting a direction. [When] you establish the policies, you start to drive black and white decisions that takes judgement calls away from leaders and, ultimately, what we want to have in our company is 6,000 leaders not 6,000 doers.

He offers an example of how strong values can be more effective than a list of rules. A few years ago the company quite reasonably decided to improve standards of health and safety and did so by establishing a set of rules and procedures, but these changes resulted in the decision to terminate some high-performing, long-standing employees who had violated the policy no more than a couple of times. The person who led the manufacturing division came to see me and said:

> Hey, listen. I understand what we're trying to do, but I'm losing really good people. I don't think it makes sense because in those cases where people violated company policy they believed that what they were doing benefitted their fellow employees and their customers. So we decided that this policy had to be adjusted, to be made broader. We needed our leaders to have the flexibility to use their own judgement in making decisions, and we delivered additional safety training to assist them do that. When you take judgement away from leaders you stop them from being leaders and they become managers, when what we really want is leaders. Leaders have to make difficult calls and they won't always be clear and they won't always be comfortable to make.

The Living Office concept

The basic idea behind Herman Miller's *Living Office* concept is to overturn the idea that regards offices as being like the factory floor in the 1960s and 1970s. The workplace now is hyper-connected and a great deal of activity is knowledge-driven. As a consequence, much greater attention is needed to create ergonomically sensitive, well-planned creative places. Much more is now being driven by creativity and problem-solving than rote process. 'That's not to say that process is not needed in the office,' says Brian Walker:

> We use a lot of our Herman Miller productivity system techniques in the office, but we also believe that we are heading into an age where the office is going to have to be rethought as a place of creativity and innovation, a place that people are attracted to. The lines are going to blur between the way people live and the way people work.

[The Living Office concept] really started with the basic idea of saying, 'If we can understand the type of work that you do, the kind of culture that you have and if we can understand the way that you need to do that (we call it your modes of work) we can then determine what kind of setting you need throughout your day to be able to be the most productive in those modes of work.' We believe that if you are thoughtful about this process it will not only result in a higher satisfaction rate from your people, but it will also result in lower operating costs for the business and a higher degree of innovation.

We believe if you can put all those things together you will ultimately create a system of prosperity that is based on an idea of abundance rather than scarcity. When people look at their facilities they come at it from a point of view of saying, 'we can improve productivity, interaction etc. by designing living office concepts that reduce costs. These new spaces will be better, more productive spaces that your people [will] love more. It will also create a sense of purpose for your organization'.

A move towards organizations that are more purpose driven

Brian Walker detects a movement towards companies and organizations that are more purpose-driven, with a new generation of consumers and employees who not only believe that what they buy is important, but that the companies they buy them from are equally important, as is their impact on the world:

This can be seen in the *start-up culture* which has greater tendency for people to move from company to company looking for more than just the pay. They want to know that their work has meaning. I often say that, at Herman Miller, we're trying to move from having transactions to having relationships, and from having places where people come to visit us to having experiences. We're trying to move from having customers to having fans and we're trying to move from having employees to having owners. I think you have to see those things as an inter-related set of activities and I think you have to be authentic. Having authenticity is as important as having purpose because if your leaders don't believe it people will uncover you very quickly.

AKQA – United Kingdom

Create an environment for people to be happy and successful

AKQA is a brand experience agency with twenty-one studios worldwide. It is a relatively young company, having been founded by Ajaz Ahmed and James Hilton in the 1990s. It has grown rapidly as the disciplines of marketing and data science converge in the age of the internet and social media. Sam Kelly, Managing Director, said:

> A bigger part of business, alongside the work and the commercials, are the people. If the people are happy and enthusiastic and are working on great work, and have the environment to do it in as well, this creates a culture of success. It's a fairly simple, straightforward model, but it requires constant reiteration and constant care. [It's about] working with teams of people – the right people – and working towards that common goal, and making sure that our people have the freedom to be the very best at what they can be.

Digital innovation and the enthusiastic mindset of young people

Digital communications are transforming the business world. The millennial generation has grown up with an expectation of being able to connect with people globally and to find ideas that inspire, not just follow a career. They do not respond well to being micro-managed. If you look at young people today, one of the big things is their desire to create ideas that have a purpose. They all have this energy and they all have this hope that they can make the world a better place, that their voice will be heard and that they'll work with great people just like them. I think there's a lot of businesses out there that are still at Level 3, even Level 2, who need to embrace where technology can take them, as well as the young people who will take them there.

Culture plays the key part

Nurturing the right culture in the workplace is now a central responsibility for businesses and key to this is a high level of good quality communication. You cannot communicate enough and you cannot listen enough. We constantly listen on a daily basis, communicating where we're going as a business while giving people the chance to present and share their thoughts as well. That reflects one of the big *shifts* from Level 3 to Level 4.

AKQA initiatives: perfected induction

AKQA places much emphasis on getting the employment experience right, which begins with the induction. When you join AKQA you know that you've joined the company you want to work for. You go home and tell everyone you know about it, you have had one of those 'Instagram' moments. What is the feeling you have after being here for half-an-hour? Do you feel like you are a person? [Do you feel] that your desk is set up? Do you feel that you've met everyone in the team? Do you go out for lunch and socialize with your new colleagues? Do you feel that you understand the business, its values and what you need to do to succeed? Do you feel that you know what the *purpose* is?

Bring the team together

Bonding the team is more than just sharing work-related activities. The business has a saying, 'the family that eats together stays together'. So we created a sense of community, which is essential to reach Level 4 performance. We do at least one thing a week that pulls the team together. We have Friday breakfast at the beginning of the month – for everybody – and we always change the theme so it's a constant reinvention. At the end of the month we do a business update where we update people on current business activities and the work that's being done in London and around the world. We also inform our people about how we're changing the business – based on their feedback.

We also do *AKQA Insight.* This [presentation] happens once a month. The last presentation we had was delivered by the head of astronaut relations for Virgin Galactic. These presentations vary wildly, from the arts to the sciences to motivational speakers, to cyber psychologists and to globally-renowned chefs. We believe that expanding peoples' cultural awareness and exposing them to the arts and sciences is another way to inspire our teams. We also showcase artists who are based at AKQA. By understanding what is going on in the world, the teams broaden their mindsets.

Real time review and feedback

The employee commitments are our version of 'Virgin Unites 100% Human' initiative,[1] which happens at least once a month for twenty-five people from the business. They share information across six key points on how they feel and as well as speak about those things they would like to change. This enables managers to take those comments on board and make changes.

We have now moved to a real-time review process where people can now immediately share feedback with each other on their projects and on other people's performance. We now have an ongoing pulse rather than a yearly review and it seems alien to the millennials that some businesses hold reviews just once every 365 days and that decisions are then made as a result of that one review.

Move from vertical to inspirational leadership

Sam Kelly added:

One thing we do that is really important is our *Defining Moments* programme, which gives every employee the opportunity to sit with myself and Ajaz, our CEO, and learn about the DNA of AKQA. What is our purpose? What is our vision? What does great work look like?

I think if you're going to move from Level 3 to Level 4, [what] you need to hear is: Who are you working for? What does it stand for? Where are we going as business? How can you contribute to the success of that and to the success of my own career? I think that is vitally important especially when the generation that is coming through is desperate to make the world a better place.

Kelly meets every new employee after they have been with AKQA for three months. He sits down with them and asks, 'What would you change about us?' The ideas that emerge from these meetings prompt ideas for innovations in our services and to our ways of working.

Create a culture that is listening and responding and adapting

There's no point in doing it if you're just listening and people don't see any difference. That's when people start to say, 'What's the point?' That is the whole point of constant communication, 'You've said this, we've changed that, you would like this, we're going to do that, and this is how you can help us get there.'

My thought [on one occasion] was, well, on a nice day why don't we surprise our employees by giving them a picnic hamper (one that includes wine). They can take an extra hour for lunch and go off for two hours. Everyone picks up their picnic hamper, finds a beautiful park and takes three people with them, people in the business who you may not know. They just go to the park to enjoy a picnic. The whole park is then filled with people and picnic hampers. People who have just met one another begin to share stories about AKQA and who they are. This was just one of those small things that doesn't cost a fortune, and it's generally the small things that mean the most.

Management training and development

People hired by AKQA tend to be highly ambitious and have an enthusiastic mind-set that is set at Level 4. They are potential leaders. They want to be informed about the company's direction. Employees ask questions such as, what is the direction we're going in? How can you help me get there? How are you going to train me, teach me and inspire me?' (There is a big focus on management training with a full training and development plan for all employees.) The new people coming in have a belief that, for them, anything is achievable, that they want to make the world a better place, that they want to do meaningful work, but they also want you to help educate them. Then I will do the best I can for them.

Results

Kelly finds that when people have an elevated sense of pride in where they work, their work output is of a higher quality. People enjoy coming to work and know that the work they're doing is making a difference to society and culture and to the quality of life of customers. He added:

> There are three things that I always say you can put in place that will help the company. First, create a great environment to work in. Second, the work has to be meaningful. Third, ensure that the people coming into the business have the right mindset? If you get those three things right – a great environment, great work and the right mindset – I think you start to hit Level 4 and Level 5.

Founder Ajaz Ahmed added:

> I think the language of business is going through a *shift*. The narrative (or lexicon) used to be efficiency, productivity, profit and growth, but now the words that really matter are purpose, beauty and optimism. To us leadership means one thing, which is to be a decent human being. At AKQA we're

trying to simplify the business as much as possible while trying to make it more understandable and less mechanized.

Royal Dutch Shell – the Netherlands

Royal Dutch Shell is one of the largest and longest established oil and petrochemical companies in the world. Given the fluctuations in oil price and the increasing controversy over the use of fossil fuels, oil companies are facing volatile conditions both politically and in the marketplace. Kalyan Ram Madabhushi, Global General Manager, says that the organization is alert to the need to engage with its stakeholders, customers and staff, and it must continually reinvent itself.

Key beliefs for pursuing core purpose

Throughout the last twenty-five years, my core purpose has been to make a difference in whatever role I embark on. In the oil and petrochemical industry, it is my deep conviction that making the world a safer, more environmentally friendlier place is also good business. The key beliefs that have helped me thus far are:

1 Deliver results through inspiration rather than desperation. Inspire people who are energized to look beyond their [own] basic needs to deliver results, rather than have people work harder because they lose something if they fail.

2 Contentment with ambition. Be content and happy with what you have today, but have the ambition to improve and be better tomorrow.

3 Acknowledge that real ambitions and dreams can only be realized if you exhibit a certain level of selflessness.

The focus you had in *The Management Shift* – on the transition from traditional organizations to enthusiastic individuals and collaborative organizations – resonates completely. From my experience, I think it's quite difficult to excel and get breakthrough performances at every level without moving beyond traditional management strictures. With Level 3, we can still survive and we can still do well, but if you aspire to be number one, or if you want to be a pathfinder, getting to Level 4/5 is essential.

Key questions to ask each employee

Shell recognized the importance of making a fundamental *shift* in employees' mindsets and behaviours. Each of us, individually, holds the key to unlocking the energy in the organization. We came up with something called *iMindset*. *iMindset* is about finding that inner motivation and inspiration that connects us to the choices we make and the behaviours we demonstrate. To get to the level of *iMindset*, we asked everyone in the organization to consider the three following questions:

1   What inspires you to be the best you can be? Do you know which of your personal attributes connect with the organizations direction and values?

2   What can you do every day in order for the team to improve and win?

3   What can teams collaboratively do every day to win?

Results

Each business unit within the Shell Group finds that it is able to attract top talent more easily, which creates traction in other parts of the group. However, each business unit must realize that they need to identify those certain core principles that inspire people and tailor those principles to their respective environments. We need to be able to:

1   Attract extremely good talent. The best people give you the best results.

2   Maintain an aligned, collective purpose.

3   Display creativity and Innovation.

Our employees must create and inspire a sense of urgency to be a pathfinder, and find the courage to make difficult choices.

Lockheed Martin – UK

Lockheed Martin is the largest defence corporation in the world. Stephen Ball was the CEO of their UK division when he was interviewed for this project. With his extensive knowledge of the famous *Skunkworks* teams – small groups of people working in innovative and often unconventional ways – he described what it takes to make a high-performing organization operate at Level 4, and sometimes at Level 5. It is all about focusing on the mission while creating the conditions and the environment for high-performing mindsets and behaviours:

> Is it just that we have the Lockheed Martin logo on the front gate when people walk into the business? Does it feel like a Lockheed Martin business in terms of the way people think and the way they behave?

Mission-led business command versus task command

Stephen explained the importance of focusing on the 'mission' to achieve high performance:

> I believe it is about having a strong sense of mission, putting people into the right environment and making it clear to them what you aspire to, and make them want to be part of it as well. The Level 3 command and control culture just doesn't do that.
>
> I've always been a strong believer in mission-led businesses rather than task command. Task command enables people *not* take responsibility because they say, 'Well I did your task. I knew it was stupid, but I did it

because you told me to,' whereas mission leadership empowers people and gives them a sense of ownership in the outcome. 'People are empowered when they are given a mission and the responsibility to execute that mission. They are then allowed to figure out for themselves as to how they will achieve it.'

In his administration team, for example, they elect their own leader and are given the mission against which they are to be measured, but they are able to decide how they organize themselves. 'This makes the team the *architects of the solution*,' he says. 'All that senior managers have to do is help them with the tools.'

> With task command we wouldn't have achieved the step-change improvements or the growth and success that we've achieved. We just couldn't have done it, because in a command and control culture you rely on the intellect of the leadership alone. In the UK we have some 3,300 people, but the number of leaders amount to perhaps only ten people. Why wouldn't you leverage all of that additional intellectual capacity?

Skunkworks teams: leveraging the power of the Level 5 mindset and culture

'The power of Level 5 is well illustrated by description of how Skunkworks teams work,' he says:

> It is about not feeling constrained. What you're trying to do is to drive profound change, therefore you need to know what the parameters of change are and what drives that change.
>
> If you want to change peoples' behaviours then you need to change two things: (a) the environment you put them in and (b) their skills and abilities. Just saying, 'I want you to change your behaviours,' might give you a warm

feeling, but it won't deliver an outcome. That comes only when you secure the different sets of behaviours you need.

Finally, one must instil a sense of purpose. It's about that creative process of saying to one another, 'Can we make an aircraft that is invisible? What would it take?' That is the purpose of our organization. You then start to see what the mindset *shift* is all about: a sense of purpose, identity, values and beliefs, skills and capabilities, and the environment.

You need to have a chief executive that has had a shift in mindset

Leveraging the success of Level 4 organization starts at the top:

You need to have a chief executive who has had a mindset *shift*, or who has got to that place. Then it will depend on the business and the challenges you face. My personal experience is that my own performance is much better when I'm working in a Level 4 or Level 5 environment. My personal job satisfaction, my commitment to the business, everything about my own situation is so much better. Much of [our] experience is driven by the environment we're in. We can be happy or sad because of our environment, so if you want people to be high-performing you have to put them in an environment that is going to encourage high performance.

We can't afford not to do it

It is important that leaders follow their intuition and do what feels right, and then absolutely commit to following it through. Stephen said:

I have often had people trying to derail me. Finance guys would say, 'We just can't afford this,' particularly for the project that set up the UK Skunkworks. I said, 'We can't afford not to,' with the result that we got a billion pound programme from a relatively modest investment.

At the time we were a loss-making business, but we invested money in the business and we stuck with it against the advice of some good people. If I hadn't had my own personal commitment and conviction it wouldn't have happened. It's easy to get derailed, so don't let that happen. Finally don't let it be an initiative, make it an imperative.

50 Key strategies for the *shift* in private sector corporations

Some of the barriers to moving towards a high-performing, highly-engaged workplace in the corporate sector stem from cultural mindset issues. There is a common belief that treating workers well always comes at a cost and that the hierarchical Level 3 approach is the most cost-efficient way of running a corporation. The inspirational case studies in this chapter turn these assumptions upside down. The way to gain meaningful control is by delegating effectively, and the route to superior profits is by empowering and helping workers deliver the best outcomes for their customers.

What these big-picture findings illustrate is that improved performance cannot come from better strategy, improved tactics and organizational design alone – they must be accompanied by an empowering style of leadership. The difference in mindset between Level 3 and Level 4/5, as summarized in Table 3.1, is radical – from viewing people as an exploitable resource to seeing them as whole human beings, worthy and capable of high performance. Without this change, ideally starting at the top of the organization, attempts to achieve a higher performance level are unlikely to succeed. Table 3.2 shows fifty key strategies for the *shift* in private sector corporations.

TABLE 3.2 50 Key strategies for the shift in private sector corporations

STRATEGY	CULTURE	RELATIONSHIPS	INDIVIDUALS	STRATEGY	SYSTEMS	RESOURCES
Delegating tasks so as to free time for strategic issues	√		√	√		
Adopting two key principles of self-management: (1) people shouldn't use force against others and (2) people should keep the commitments they make to others	√	√	√	√		
Adopting an entrepreneurial mindset	√		√	√	√	
Allocating areas of responsibility and taking responsibility for delivering results	√		√			
Owning all decisions (as CEO) in designated areas of responsibility			√			
Turning work into game and making it fun, e.g. give people a personal mission and create scorecards that they can use themselves and measure their own productivity and performance	√			√		√
Manage complexity through simplicity – keep things simple	√			√	√	
Give up on the illusion/delusion of control	√		√			

Description					
Use transparent information				√	√
Unlock innovation throughout the entire enterprise by giving people a voice and a stake in results	√		√	√	√
Allow people to step up as leaders, based upon their expertise and interests on issues and processes	√		√	√	√
Have two-way communication from leaders that focus on the employee's needs and passions, that are aligned with business needs, customer needs and project needs	√	√	√	√	
Commit to a clear high-level mission/purpose and deeply connect with that purpose. It is the reason for our existence	√			√	
Make connections between culture, relationships, individuals, strategy, systems and resources to create value in a more systematic and transformational way	√	√	√	√	√
Use social media (e.g. Yammer) to create inclusive groups for collaboration and the exchange of ideas among diverse groups of employees. Grow a social movement by connecting to other networks	√	√		√	

(Continued)

TABLE 3.2 (*Continued*)

STRATEGY	CULTURE	RELATIONSHIPS	INDIVIDUALS	STRATEGY	SYSTEMS	RESOURCES
Use the power of stakeholder engagement	√			√		
Use self-organizing, non-hierarchical teams and purpose-based communities	√	√		√	√	
Create collaborative alliances of partners		√		√		
Enthuse and empower those people who create value for customers and who best understand customer needs	√	√	√	√		
As step one, create significant dissatisfaction with the status quo				√		
Create a clear vision for tomorrow, a vision that is so compelling that everybody jumps up from their bed and goes to work to achieve that vision	√		√	√		
Experiment with ways to achieve a new vision in a fast and inexpensive way				√	√	
Allow customer-facing employees to make decisions			√	√		
Focus on customer satisfaction	√		√	√		

Remove absolute goals, but strive to do better than your peers	√				√	
Be cost-efficient, have lower costs than your peers	√				√	√
Move away from short-term thinking	√			√	√	
Take the change initiative down to the operational level	√			√	√	
Communicate regularly through different channels		√			√	
Use story-telling	√				√	
Find the model that empowers people and a structure that works	√				√	
Ensure that there is transparency and openness	√				√	
Give autonomy to employees to set their own goals and establish processes to measure these goals	√		√		√	
Provide ways for employees to make suggestions and share ideas for innovation, and take action when appropriate	√				√	√

(Continued)

TABLE 3.2 (Continued)

STRATEGY	CULTURE	RELATIONSHIPS	INDIVIDUALS	STRATEGY	SYSTEMS	RESOURCES
Produce sustainable change with small steps that have been practiced over time, with feedback and peer support	√			√	√	
Build meaningful relationships and make work visible with the use of technology		√		√	√	√
Practice purposeful discovery and a growth mindset	√		√			
Use profit sharing incentives and perks for staff. These improve customer engagement and profit				√	√	√
Manage by principles, where everybody is a leader	√		√	√		
Be authentic in today's transparent internet world	√		√			
Create an environment for people to be happy and successful through constant reiteration	√		√			
Ensure that employees' voices are heard, and take actions as a result	√		√	√	√	
Enable ongoing real time review and feedback	√			√	√	
Move from a vertical to an inspirational leadership, communicating the vision and purpose continuously	√		√	√		

Description			
Create a culture that is listening, responding and adapting	√		√
Show a level of care by doing little things for employees (e.g. picnic baskets on sunny days)	√	√	√
Understand that it is down to each individual to unlock the energy in the organization. Ask employees, 'What can you do every day in order for the team to improve and win? What can the teams do collaboratively every day?'	√	√	√
Deliver results through inspiration rather than desperation. Inspire those people who are energized to look beyond their basic needs to deliver results (rather than make people work harder because they lose something if they fail to achieve)	√	√	
Be contented and happy with what you have today, but have the ambition to improve and be better tomorrow		√	
Ask your employees, 'What inspires you to be the best you can be, every day? Do you understand how your personal values connect with the organization's direction and values?'		√	√

(Continued)

SEVEN REFLECTION POINTS FROM THIS CHAPTER

1 Beyond making money, does your business have a strong and engaging sense of purpose?

2 Have you learned to address the mindset within yourself and that of your leadership team?

3 Do you see employees as colleagues who co-create value rather than resources whose cost should be minimized?

4 Do you see communication throughout the enterprise as being at the heart of what you do, rather than a strategic necessity and a daily discipline?

5 Do you take responsibility for the impact you can make? For example, by beginning initiatives to move to Level 4 even when the context is not encouraging?

6 Do you build constituencies of like-minded people as you seek to create change?

7 Do you treat management of performance as a daily discipline that should not be postponed until the yearly appraisal?

4

Entrepreneurial rising stars getting it right: Inspirational stories from SMEs

KEY INSIGHTS FROM THIS CHAPTER

- A highly-participative, entrepreneurial Level 4 is easier to instil in a start-up than it is to bring about change in a large organization.
- Many smaller new starts have maintained this high-performing way of working and found that it helped them to grow.
- Some of the most innovative firms have radically rewritten the ways of doing business, even abolishing rules for days off and job titles.
- High levels of trust are necessary for maintaining this type of culture.

An enlightened entrepreneurial mindset is aligned with a Level 4 mindset

It is common to talk about the need for more entrepreneurial ways of running businesses, not least because we live in an unpredictable world. Command and control hierarchical corporations used to project a degree of stability in the markets and they used technology that is now obsolete, but what does an entrepreneurial way of working actually entail and how can businesses nurture and sustain it? This is a challenge for every enterprise, new and old, large and small. The evidence linking leadership ability and high performance is every bit as relevant for Uber as it is for IBM, because it is still about dealing with people and relationships.

What we have learned is that moving up the levels of the *Management Shift* is crucial. We have also learned that this is behavioural and multi-dimensional. One must monitor and nurture attitudes and abilities and pay heed to the organizational structure. This chapter features stories and insights from those empowering leaders in small and medium-sized enterprises who took part in this research. One of the common traits that these leaders share is a Level 4 mindset – an ability and a commitment to work collaboratively for the common good, focusing on people and purpose, and by doing good by doing well at the same time.

Propellernet – UK

Propellernet is a digital marketing agency based in Brighton in the UK. Its founder, Jack Hubbard, lives with his family and manages the company from his home in the French Alps. He wanted to set up and run his own company because, as an employee, he found it difficult to find a workplace culture he was comfortable working in.

When he began hiring, he initially found it challenging and one of his early lessons was to learn to place emphasis on the attitude and mindset of applicants rather than basing hiring decisions on obvious personal skills and the content of a CV. When recruiting in the digital marketing industry specifically, he faced intense competition from other companies who were also trying to recruit the best staff – and the competition offered higher salaries. Thus, retention of staff became a priority. Jack wanted to appeal to applicants on more than just the issue pay:

I always believed that if people were giving up their time and commitment to buy into our vision, I felt that I needed to return that to them in some way. I never felt very comfortable being the boss. I just tried to be friends with everyone and looked after everyone, and I hoped that they would want to look after the company.

He found that whenever he and his employees followed their values, which they articulated as having fun, personal well-being, innovation, creativity and adventure, everything else took less effort. It was easier to achieve their objectives this way, rather than by following an approach based on spreadsheets and hitting the numbers, guided by exhaustively defined micro-initiatives:

[The latter] is a much more mechanical kind of approach, but when we began to let go of that and started to just operate in accordance to our values and purpose, it kind of freed us up a lot more. We became a lot more creative. The innovation stepped up a level. We were able to deliver while having great relationships with our clients.

In our industry it's very unusual for employees to turn up at nine o'clock and leave at five. [In other companies] people would often stay until eleven o'clock, perhaps midnight, and it was common for their billable hours to be calculated at 120% of their (standard) working day. In comparison, we never bill out our peoples time beyond seventy to eighty per cent of their standard hours. If we did otherwise, it would just burn people out.

We've got a big queue of people at the door because we go to extreme lengths to look after our staff [and] to say thank you to them for looking after us. It's not that difficult. When you decide that that's the right strategy to follow, to really look after people, coming up with innovative ideas isn't difficult because most other people aren't doing that!

Making employees dreams come true

Jack set up a wellbeing fund to enable anyone who wanted to do something interesting or fun (that was related to wellbeing) to finance their passion from the fund. There is also a *Dream Ball Machine*, which was set up to enable people to do things they've always wanted to do. Each ball contains someone's name and their dream. When the company meets its monthly targets, the *Ball* is used to reveal someone's name and their dream. Examples include flying employees to Brazil for the World Cup and booking a ski chalet for a week for a family. Jack added:

> I get quite impatient as well. I don't always want to wait until a target is hit to make someone's dream come true, so I'm always looking down the list of dreams and seeing what I can make happen anyway, regardless of the target. Particularly for the people who are really putting their heart and soul into Propellernet.

One example enabled an employee, Mark, to see the creation of his vivid and original idea for a dystopian futuristic story featuring corruption in the music industry. The storyline followed was based on an industry was that was taken over by corporate sponsors and rebels, known as Red Stars, who recorded independent albums on another planet. Jack helped Mark not merely to convert the concept into a book, but put together a group of artists, musicians, designers, comic book illustrators and actors to bring the concept to life.

In Dream Valley, at Jack's base in the Alps, the company organized a music festival called *Slope-Off*. Anyone who was a DJ, in a band, or had something to perform, was offered stage time at the venue. At the closing party, the corporate sponsor, who was an actor hired to perform a cringe-worthy sponsor's thank you speech, was kidnapped by other actors (who were dressed as Red Stars), and was then bundled him into a car. This happened just prior to the concluding show. As well as being tremendously fun and engaging in itself, these events encouraged creativity, generated a positive brand image and made contacts that helped the business.

The dream of one employee, Sophie, was to go on safari. Propellernet connected with a Namibian tour operator called Wild Dog Safaris, who needed marketing assistance themselves. So, Propellernet formed a joint venture with Wild Dog Safaris whereby Propellernet built a web presence for them that was designed to inspire more people to go to Namibia and to go on safari tours. At the time of writing, Sophie was due to spend an eight week sabbatical, to be joined later by Jack, his wife Linda and some Wild Dog Safari staff. This was for Jack's fortieth birthday celebrations.

There is a huge sea change happening within organizations

It's not easy when the rest of the business world is doing things one way and you don't believe that and you're trying to do things differently. It's easy for people to say you're crazy or it'll never work, but we were getting more and more comfortable with our way, and it seems that we were not alone. For years we didn't really connect or share these stories, we just kind of got on with it, but now I'm seeing that other people have got similar philosophies and I believe there's a huge sea change happening out there.

The move to the Alps was a radical relocation for him and his family, but it's not a semi-retirement retreat. As well as the music festival, he has arranged a series of events such as business groups hiking and staying over in the mountains as well as adventure days under the concept of Dream Valley Projects. One activity was an informal meeting, an *un-conference* if you like, for entrepreneurs from different parts of the world. The combined outdoor activities and discussions created 'this wealth of wisdom and knowledge and experience that was just bubbling up as and when it was required, based on free-flowing conversations.' At the end everyone was just like 'Wow, that was

100 times more powerful than going to a traditional conference' where you only receive a thinly-veiled sales pitches.

Just drop it and just be human!

As it's become more and more clear to us, and as we've allowed ourselves to operate in a way that feels more natural, and as we've seen the business becoming more and more successful, our confidence has grown and we've acted more in that way. If we'd acted this way at the beginning, people might have thought we were crazy or, maybe, we didn't have much confidence, but now it's like 'Just drop it and just be human!'

The result

Since the shift to Level 4 the financial performance has been incredible. Over the last four years our turnover has increased from £1.5 million to £4million. Our profits have increased from £500,000 two years ago to £600,000 last year. This year we made £600,000 profit and, on top of that, we invested £500,000 into a tech' start-up. So with a £4million turnover, we're now making effectively £1million net profit.

Measuring happiness

The company has a simple system for tracking employees' happiness. They use a weekly sad or happy face indicator. This is tracked via a dashboard where everyone can see whether it has been a happy week, or not:

We've seen the *shift* happen. It's all well and good the management team understanding what we are trying to do, but you also need it the *shift* from the bottom up and having those communication points through the systems really helps.

Nonetheless, he's not a fan of a high level of data collection:

I tend to go more by the vibes, the feeling, the culture and other indicators that people are performing well. People don't want to leave, people recommend their friends to come to work at Propellernet, and I know for sure they could leave and go and get paid more elsewhere, but they don't want to because they love the journey that they're on. Retention and performance are huge indicators.

His priority is to maintain the philosophy of enjoyment, freedom and security, as well as the realization of dreams that inspire people. The metrics that the company does use – financials, happiness levels, retention and engagement – have increased substantially since the *shift*.

Leveraging the playful spirit

There is a marked difference between an open culture where people feel encouraged to discuss and cooperate and a closed Level 3 organization. He finds:

If you're closed, if you just want to sit in your pod just repeating the same stuff again and again – which is how it used to be before the *shift* and which is how it will be if everyone has got their job description and they're all working a certain number of hours – it becomes mechanical and you don't have the kind of creativity that leads to innovation. At that point you're dead, particularly in this kind of industry, well, in any kind of industry.

The pace of change is accelerating and whole industries are being left behind. Unless you can get excited about something and embrace change with a playful attitude and try to figure out the next thing, then you're going to get wiped out. I think if you are the leader you have to lead yourself in that way and you have to read less industry news. I think you have to read less [about], 'What's this competitor doing?' Worry less about the outside world and you will be a little bit more connected to yourself as a human being.

When dealing with a dilemma, it often helps to escape from the office and go for a long walk or engage in some other activity while your *internal supercomputer* works on the problem. This can be hard to define and explain, because of the role of the subconscious.

These matters are discussed in the book, *Blink*, by the influential thinker Malcolm Gladwell. A common point of many successful leaders is that they respect and trust the subconscious and often find it difficult to fully articulate the reasons for their success.

The price tag

It may seem that the lessons of Jack Hubbard's success at Propellernet are relevant only for small, creative firms, but Jack has telling insights for larger companies:

> The issue with plc's, I guess, is that their mandate is to increase shareholder value, where everything can be measured by a spreadsheet. All of the intangibles, such as relationships, wellbeing and creativity are invisible to spreadsheets, so decisions are made without essential information. That's a huge problem, because the people who make those decisions aren't getting the information they need. They're not working in an environment where this other information is made available to them.
>
> It is obviously easier for an owner/manager in an independent business to be aware of such intangibles because they know all or most of their staff. Leaders of larger businesses are making a fundamental error if they believe that knowledge about people and relationships is unimportant, or if they fail to create a culture of creativity and innovation. Performance is important, but because plc's don't have all the information they need they make terrible decisions and create terrible work cultures. Corporations urgently need to find ways of gaining reliable information on climate and culture and incorporate that information into their decision-making processes.

FIGURE 4.1 *Propellernet's Vision Mountain (reprinted with the permission of Jack Hubbard).*

Figure 4.1 is a visual illustration of Jack Hubbard's philosophy, i.e. the success of a sustainable organizational rests upon a foundation of wellbeing, fun and creativity. If you are just starting out on the quest to reach Level 4, he advises:

Find some friends, find some other people who are going through it – it's lonely. Get a group of people who are trying to do this at the same time that you are, where you all have your own companies. Meet up once a month for inter-personal therapy. Have coffee and discuss what you're going through. It will then become less lonely and you will get support along the way. Just connect to a community of like-minded people. There's a growing community out there who are doing this kind of thing. There are a growing number of events where you can go to learn about this kind of stuff, so you need to surround yourself as much as possible with the kind of influences that make it easier for you to go on that journey.

Brand Velocity – USA

Brand Velocity is a management consultancy based in Atlanta, USA. It was set up in 2001 by a former CIO of Coca-Cola, Jack Bergstrand. It became a working laboratory on how to best organize for the *Knowledge Age*, which was inspired by Peter Drucker's book, *Post-Capitalist Society*[1] Its conclusions about Level 4 leadership were chronicled in my previous book, *The Management Shift*, so I returned to the company a couple of years later to talk to Jack about the progress that has been made since then.

Shifting to Level 4

When asked for an overview of the benefits of Level 4 leadership and the results of working with the *Management Shift* principles, Jack replied:

> Organizationally, we were able to make the shift from Level 3 to Level 4, which resulted in greater enthusiasm and collaboration. This resulted in the company increasing its growth trajectory and being named by Consulting magazine as a consulting jewel. There is no doubt that we could not have made the connections between culture, relationships, individuals, strategy, systems and resources to create value in a more systematic and transformational way [without using *the Management Shift* approach]. As a company we became much more collaborative [and we] institutionalized a unique compensation and rewards practice. We also implemented specific collaboration tools, which created a work environment with greater personal freedom.

Management innovation

Some of the innovative management practices implemented included the following:

1 Using a points-based rather than a hierarchical-based compensation
   system. Anyone in the company can earn more money than their boss

if they sell or deliver great work, or if they recruit and develop people who can do that.

2   Compensation is transparent. Every employee is able to access financial statements and other corporate records.

3   The company has implemented a virtual organizational structure. While corporate infrastructure, such as email, accounting, and payroll is standardized and handled centrally, personal infrastructure such as phones and computers are managed by the individual, as long as the decisions made are secure and support collaboration.

4   Brand Velocity has worked closely with the Drucker Institute to help it to achieve its socially-focused mission, which is 'to strengthen organizations to strengthen society'.

5   Trust is achieved through shared values, a common process, transparent measures and institutionalized communication routines.

Brand Velocity has enjoyed significant growth and strong levels of profitability since its formation. It was nominated as one of the Seven Small Jewels by *Consulting* magazine as one of the hidden gems of the consulting profession.

Obelisk–UK

Obelisk, founded by Dana Denis-Smith, is a specialist company based in London that was set up to provide remote contract work for female lawyers who have children. It has won numerous awards:

There's a central office and then there's a lot of consultants. Eighty per cent of the contractors are women. In the central team, we are all women. Our role is to bring [in] the work, to manage the work and to recruit. I always say that we should encourage our clients to prefer working with our contractors remotely, but, as you know, that's a more difficult management structure. They [the clients] naturally push back and say, 'Actually, I want to have a body in the office,' but we always try and explain that they get better value if they're more relaxed about where people work.

Flexible working is the future

A lot of our people are mums who aren't able to work full-time, but they do want to work flexibly. That's another challenge for our clients. This structure doesn't mean that the work is not going to be done, it's just going to be done in a different way. Sometimes we have a job explaining to our clients that they can have what they want, but there are still occasions when they just want things done the traditional way.

I started from the basis of asking potential contract lawyers, 'What is the time you're prepared to give?' By asking these questions and comparing and aligning our time frames with those of the contract lawyers, I could determine whether the proposed relationship was feasible.

What has been the impact of Obelisk so far?

I guess the income has had the biggest impact. You know, they [the lawyers] would not earn what they're earning now if it wasn't for us. That's the most inspiring example of the impact. I think, for me, [this is] the way of the future and the way people will work going forward. I think this is definitely the way because you're maximizing the best resource they can bring.

La Fosse Associates – UK

La Fosse Associates is a recruitment agency based in London. It was established in 2007 and now has ninety employees. As described by Simon La Fosse, the approach to establishing Level 4 leadership is to keep matters simple, with a tight focus on hiring people with the right mindset:

> One of the basic premises of management and leadership used to be that you had to spend a lot of time telling people what to do, whereas if you have highly capable people with the right values and mindsets you don't really need to tell them what to do in the same way. You need to give them a framework within which to operate and a collective sense of how we like to do stuff and, after that, you let them get on with it.
>
> We do not recruit people who are good enough. We recruit people who are exceptional. Undesirable behaviour tends to stem from having the wrong values and that is a key consideration in the hiring process, and a key factor when monitoring performance. The critical thing, the difference between outperforming a competitor and the difference between success and failure, is the quality of [your] people.

Treat people like human beings

Simon reports that many people who have been through recruitment agencies do not feel that they were treated well. La Fosse is underpinned by the business opportunities that flow from the concept of radically improving the candidate's experience in the recruitment process. This means treating all individuals well, not just those whom the agency successfully places.

Create an environment that is a pleasure to work in

The other key piece of advice is to treat people well because in sales-driven environments, which recruitment businesses essentially are, there is fierce competition and it's very easy for the competition to become more focused, both externally and internally.

If we extend the same value system to our colleagues, we will then enjoy working there even more and, if you think about it, you work five days out of seven so you spend more time with your colleagues than you do with your family. When you realize that, you realize the importance of creating a working environment where it's a pleasure to work.

Remove the divide between management and workers

There has been a conscious effort to reduce the difference in status and the difference in treatment between managers and workers. He added:

One of the reasons for the divide, certainly in the recruitment industry, is that, typically, the senior people in the organization hold a disproportionate amount of the equity, with the result that they are building capital value in addition to the money they were taking out of the company in the form of salaries and dividends. This situation continues to the point when the company is floated on the stock market and it is those senior people who benefit disproportionately from the value that has been created. There is not much left over or handed out to the ninety per cent of the organization that was driving the value.

I just thought, 'What's an appropriate and a fair amount for me to take as the risk-taker, as the person that started it?' It felt like sixty per cent, which left forty per cent for other people.'

Provide share options for people who join

He informed all members of staff that the plan was to share forty per cent of the wealth that was created by the people who helped build the company:

That fundamentally created a different perspective, one where people were not working just for themselves. They were now working toward the common good and that, I think, has been a significant part of our success and will continue to drive the business forward. Importantly, it hasn't just gone to only those people who joined me at the start of the business, share options are available to people when they join. It is no longer *them and us*, there is a sense of *we're all in it together* and it feels fundamentally fairer. The consequence of that is we get a lot more discretionary effort, a lot more loyalty and a lot more people caring about the brand and the reputation of the company.

The thing that has developed over time is a clear sense of purpose and an understanding that we stand for something different, and that, collectively, we are developing a business that treats people in a fundamentally different way to previously accepted business practices. What really excites us is that by doing [as we are doing] and achieving commercial success, others will follow [our lead] and change the dynamics of the recruitment industry. This will then have the effect of improving the treatment of hundreds of thousands of people who, when they are looking for a job, are at a vulnerable point in their lives.

Our senior managers maintain high levels of communication with their team; they also emphasize positive feedback in their quest *to catch people doing something right.*

The results from starting the company at Level 4

One tangible result of moving towards Level 4 has been a succession of 'Best Company to Work For' nominations – an accolade that adds greatly to the employer brand – and this after reaching fourth place within the first two years of entering. Other rewards include low staff turnover, with higher levels of motivation and discretionary effort. There is an understanding that people take the initiative as opposed to just following processes, knowing that that is the right thing to do for our organization.

At the time of the interview, turnover was £30 million and annual growth was thirty per cent, making it one of the 100 fastest growing companies in the UK for three consecutive years.

If we did not start at Level 4, I think we probably would have gone out of business. Recruitment businesses are very sensitive to downturns in the economy and within a year of setting up the business we went into one of the greatest downturns the British economy has ever seen. We grew through that, and that was when I think we realized we were onto something.

Operating at Level 4 is priceless

I think it [operating at Level 4] is priceless for two reasons: firstly (and I think this is the least important reason) it's given us a commercially successful business and, secondly, which is much more important for me, is that it, Level 4, has created a business that I fundamentally enjoy working in.

I believe that the vast majority of the people working here believe so to. You spend most of your life at work so if you can make sure that you work in the kind of environment you want to be in, then we've made a difference to your life. If your work is motivated by increasing profits, that's the end of your motivation. I would probably say, 'don't bother going down that path because I think your motivation has to be wider than that'.

Making a social and environmental impact

The company's sense of responsibility extends to society and to the wider environment. It commits to tree planting, to ensuring a carbon-neutral footprint and to maintaining a commitment to donate a minimum of one per cent of annual profits to charity. This provides about one third of the annual budget of a school in Malawi. Another charity is an inner-city school where many of the children have grown up in an environment where no one in their affinity is employed. The company works with the school, coaches the pupils, gives interview practices and so on to assist the pupil's chances of gaining future employment.

Crisp Consultancy – Sweden

Crisp is a consulting company based in Sweden. It has forty consultants. When one of the co-founders left in 2008, a decision was made to relaunch the company with the core aim of striving to achieve an empowering, Level 4 culture of leadership. The concept was to create a sense of common purpose and to increase the happiness and engagement of the consultants. Values became clearer and they found that decision-making became more effective. As with La Fosse recruitment, leaders at Crisp argue that the move to Level 4 was far from being a luxury or a nice-to-have extra. According to Michael Göthe, it was fundamental to the company's survival and prosperity.

Rotating the CEO role and electing board members

Before the *shift*, the company had an external CEO, i.e. a specialist executive who was not a consultant. As part of the move to creating a more participative culture, Crisp switched to a system that rotated the position of CEO. Then they moved toward an even more democratic set up. It was decided that since the role of the CEO was merely a function, it could be split to into other roles. Now there is no single CEO. The board is elected by all constituents with major decisions being taken by everyone together at a conference. Every consultant can drive any decision at any moment and there is a shared commitment to accord value to the advice of those most affected by a decision. The company is enjoying growth and seeks to boost diversity as it does so:

> Crisp has a no explicit purpose to grow, the only reason for getting new people in is to increase the level of diversity and knowledge. We think that

growing one to three persons every year is a good pace, and we want to include people who are different from us. [People] who can complement [what we do] and give new ideas and so on.

Interview people for their values and purpose

At Crisp, new consultants are interviewed about values and purpose, covering dimensions such as inner drive and motivation. Notes from these interviews are then summarized and collated, then everyone gives their feedback. This leads to discussion and modification:

> Before that, we had been trying to figure out what was the right vision, what was the right strategy and where it should go. We had different egos trying to set a direction. This was a bit frustrating, but once you actually work inside, listening to each and every person, the purpose and values became clear.

Such conversations led to the concept of treating the company like a family – it is a home for the consultants and there is a degree of freedom and autonomy based on the understanding that you care about your home and your family. The firm then moved to a new level, probably breaking new ground for a consultancy, in a quite extraordinary development. Such was the buzz and the aura about the place that the consultants started receiving requests to open offices in new cities and in different countries. Given that they wanted to stay relatively small, the company initially turned down such requests, but it did set them thinking. If software developers can freely cooperate and spread ideas through open sourcing, then why can't consultancies? So they began to encourage others to set up their own consultancies inspired by the Crisp model, which defined their approach and made it freely accessible to other consultants. This outsourced model is the DNA of Crisp. In a similar vein, Crisp encouraged spin-off projects and ideas, with consultants taking part in conferences, coaching initiatives and so on. The DNA can be found at: https://dna.crisp.se

I don't think there is any company that is not suitable for that [Level 4 way of working]. I think it will be key for managing the complexity that we're living in today as well as for managing the high levels of competition, while also thinking about young people. They don't want to be in a traditional command and control organization. There are so many *shifts* going in the same direction.

Gamevy Ltd – UK

Gamevy was created in 2013 by three founders: Paul Dolman-Darrall, Dan Rough and Helen Walton. It brings TV game shows online to a real-money audience. From the start, the founders wanted a company genuinely co-owned by all of the staff, one that had no formal hierarchy. Those two principles, which decided how the company was going to work, came before what the company was going to do. Helen Walton, a co-founder, said the principles were more important than the product itself.

Rewarding risk

The essential model is that we wanted to reward risk. Those who invest the most in a start-up, especially at the very beginning when you're unlikely to make any money and where you may be putting off rewards for a really significant amount of time, have an actual cost and an emotional cost that needs to be rewarded.

On the other hand, successful start-ups over-reward their founders and under-reward those who join later, who may have been just as important to the eventual success. We wanted to create a better balance, one that encouraged employees to feel a genuine sense of ownership and made them act like owners. If you want people to feel like owners, the best way to do that is to make them owners. You often hear lots of companies talking about employee engagement, [but] I think they spend too much effort on [these] plans when just giving ownership would be easier.

There is a set of rules which Helen describes as theoretical, at least initially. They are constantly revised and informed by experience.

Pivot point for managing distributed earnings

Among the changes that have been subjected to revision is the pay structure, e.g. judgements on what they refer to as the *pivot point*. This is the point at which the earnings of one person go over a certain, pre-defined amount. This is the point at which the company starts earning more. The person who reaches their *pivot point* no longer earns additional, incremental money as quickly as they did before, which creates a more even balance between the founding staff and those who joined later:

> It means that any person in the company who creates value can genuinely see the rewards of that value returned to them, even if they were the last person to join. They can basically increase the value of the company and benefit from that.

The rules essentially had two purposes: the founders believed that they were the right thing to do and they were a means to incentivize and motivate employees. They also kept the cost base relatively low, thus improving the company's resilience.

No bosses

The *no bosses* principle can cause confusion to outsiders since this can be interpreted as an absence of accountability or decision-making, but, as Paul Dolman-Darrall points out, this is a challenge for all types of organizational structures:

Hierarchies are often unclear as to who made the decisions in the first place, but the absence of bosses fundamentally misinterprets the power of management. Management's real power is not, in my opinion, decision-making, micromanagement is astonishingly difficult in and of itself. Instead, employees get phenomenal freedom. The idea that decisions are made by managers is a flawed notion.

In fact, shrewd management power exists somewhere else and it's predominantly to do with the level of freedom that each individual has had accorded to them. We constrain people as opposed to making decisions for them. We don't tell them what to do. Often our managers will say, 'We'll let you deal with the *how*.'

The founders, however, did provide some constraints:

We give them job titles, job descriptions and we physically locate them, but we don't give them access to money. We keep [control of] money very tight because that's a true management control, but we do try to constrain their time. Predominantly our employees own their time and have limited access to money (a maximum of ten per cent of cash reserves).

Nurture transparency and manage by dissent

The key to making this approach work is transparency. Checks and balances in the organization let other employees see what is being done and that enables them to either help or hinder, as they wish. This is not the kind of hindering in the manner of a hierarchical manager, but *hindering* through discussion:

Then it becomes a broader debate. Collaboration is not alignment, true collaboration is often not aligned. Symphony orchestras that are in constant tension, who have musicians who don't like one another and argue bitterly, often play the best music – not orchestras where everyone is in harmony, where everything's great and where everyone is happy.

We describe this as *management by dissent*. We never try to reach a consensus. What we are saying is, 'Does anyone care enough to really dissent from this, to really object to it and do something differently?' Everyone has the decision-making power and the power to carry out their own decisions. Even if everyone disagrees with you, we try to avoid group thinking and consensus. We imbue people with the power to go and do what they want to do anyway. We're not saying that hierarchy does not exist, we just allow it to form at the point of need where no pre-existing structure has formed.

Take a leadership position based on a natural flow

At Gamevy, people naturally take leadership positions based partly on their expertise, but also taking into account matters that would appear highly idiosyncratic at other organizations, such as, 'how you feel this week'. Helen added:

There are weeks when one is feeling full of energy and enthusiasm and you naturally tend to lead more. There are weeks, maybe months, when you're feeling exhausted and you need to take a rest, and then there are also questions about just how much you care about a particular thing. If you happen to care passionately about a particular product, you will lead it. People follow passion and enthusiasm.

There are some checks and balances to prevent the 'no bosses' set-up becoming anarchic. For most situations, these involve discussion and communication rather than a set of rules. For example, if a project reaches a certain size, the company then hosts a conversation around the question, 'Can this continue?' This approach encourages innovation and experimentation. For extreme, crisis-type situations a leader is immediately assigned to take quick decisions, decisions that would normally take too long to achieve by way of discussion. Helen draws a comparison to a ship that is sinking, but she also points out that such instances in business are 'astonishingly rare'. She added:

> We say trust is assumed. You can lose trust, at which point our relationship almost certainly ends, but we begin by gifting trust. You don't have to earn it, it's given at the beginning. I would argue that organizations with low trust will probably use the word trust a lot, whereas organizations with high trust just don't use it – they don't use it – they don't need to.

Measuring the impact

Profitability per employee is a key measure and the reason it is important is because it is connected to employee ownership:

> Every time you take on a new person, you're essentially saying to yourself, 'Is employing them going to grow the value of the company to such an extent that diluting my ownership share is worth it?' These are the kinds of decisions that we take every time we hire someone, and it's a key thing. As we know, a lot of companies spend company money as if it doesn't really matter, including, by the way, companies that are the most obsessed with shareholder value. They have a fairly low personal investment in how money gets spent. We hold the opposite view, the money belongs to the employees and one must be very clear that when spending it you must do so to increase value.

Limitations of hierarchies

The philosophy is not to be anti-management per se, Paul adds:

> I don't necessarily reject the idea that management work still exists. I just reject the idea that it has to be done by managers. Instead, our management work, the bits of it that do exist, are done by or shared by everybody in the company. I think we all know of companies where short-term decisions

made by directors are sometimes in the interests of shareholders, and sometimes not. This can lead to profitability just diving.

It starts with the CEO. It's not that you can't become more innovative, it's not that you can't increase trust and it's not that you can't increase collaboration, but the idea that a CEO can make massive changes to an organization when they are only prepared to defend their own vested interest is nonsense. Every now and then a radical thinker who becomes the CEO can change it, and it is here one can see that a CEO has a phenomenal power to initiate change, but to do so they must allocate the responsibility for making those changes to the very people that they're constraining. Paradoxically, this suits their own vested interest.

While hierarchies can be efficient at running large organizations in markets where demand is stable, the organization can become highly vulnerable when a disruptive competitor enters the market. The rate of change initiated by the competitor can out-accelerate the rate of change that can be achieved by a hierarchical business. One of the big problems of scale is that you can convince yourself that, 'We're too big to fail,' and then, all of a sudden, you do just that.

Cocoon Projects – Italy

Cocoon Projects, founded by Stelio Verzera, is the first European open enterprise that provides end-to-end services for evolution, value-driven organizations.

Move away from rigid structuring to survive

Stelio argues that some of the conventional concepts of business structure and development require radical redefinition. He says:

I was working in marketing innovation in 2008 when I first realized that new organizational models had to be devised and implemented. We experienced this in our own company when we were trying to get structured in order to grow. We started to apply the rigid and static structures, the tenets of which are taught in almost all business schools.

It turned out to be the wrong thing to do in one of the biggest economic crises that hit Europe sometime between 2009 and 2010. We saw that almost all of our customers suffered from that error too, getting stuck with their rigid structures and all that comes with that. They were unable to adapt to the fast-changing environment where there was people disengagement and value production paralysis. In their moments of greatest need, they couldn't move. Many of them died.

That actually happened to our company as well. We had to close it. We had employees, we were growing and we had international customers, and it was going well till that moment, but it turned out that, in this unexpected crisis, the structuring we had put in place was a big problem in itself. We had made ourselves unable to adapt fast enough.

Liquid Organisation model

So, Stelio and his team designed a new organizational model referred to as a *Liquid Organisation*:

We seriously asked ourselves, 'How would a really cool company be today? One that doesn't experience all these problems and one that makes people want to work there? One that is not just robust, but is resilient and antifragile?' We worked on the new model for nine months and we ended up with this framework, which we called *Liquid Organisation*.

First of all, we identified the space for the evolution of a human organization in three directions: openness, inclusiveness and leanness. The first, openness, is about information flow and conversations. The second, inclusiveness, is about co-creation of innovation and decision-making. It's about collective intuition, collective intelligence and collective emotional intelligence. The third, leanness, is more about operational agility, which is linked to seeking out value and eliminating waste. This is well-explained in the lean management body of knowledge and it is about collaboration between people.

We decided to push all three dimensions to the maximum extent we could, thus making radical choices in different areas. For example, by taking out what we believed were different kinds of waste. Take job interviews as an example. Why should we spend time planning or analyzing whether someone will fit into our organization when we can simply allow that person to enter the system at its heart and wait and see how this very complex relationship turns out? It is in any event a multi-layered, dynamic two-way match that depends on that particular moment in the new employee's life converging with the moment of our life as a company. We devised a framework whereby if the match didn't work people would just fade out. They didn't need anybody to fire them. Conversely, if the match worked, they stayed. To give another example on the dimension of openness, we decided to go for radical transparency. Everybody knows what's going on in our company from the day they join.

Stelio says that the company is growing well. It has a strong, shared sense of purpose and has attained the virtuous circle of having engaged people who produce strong results. The key to this philosophy has been to unify the organizational structure with a sense of purpose, rather than treat the latter as an optional extra.

The company needs to adapt to people's needs, not the other way round

Stelio works with some people who still work with other companies; some of them are entrepreneurs within their own companies. The boundaries of the company began to blur, but he has found:

As it's completely open, some of our customers have entered the governance of our company. Boundaries start to be recognized by their real nature, which is blurred while being dynamic. This is amazing, I think. The company starts to be something that naturally adapts to what people need to work well, not the reverse.

Another feature is what he calls *contribution meritocracy*, a concept directly related to that of *operational reputation*. It is a way for the company to deploy a system that is based on the concept of employee contribution, rather than a judgement on performance. There is a continual co-assessment among peers of how much each person is contributing to the value created, and this is governed by a flow of feedback loops. At the same time, transparently tracing these dynamics for anyone to see in order to enable adaptation and emergence is the way forward for a dynamic alignment of personal and ecosystemic interests.

Continuous usage of resources and continuous prioritization

We don't separate strategy from tactics anymore, it doesn't make any sense. There is a concurrent and continuous flow of inclusive strategy-making, driven by purpose, vision, values and emerging reality. We don't do up-front budgeting either. We have implemented a system for the continuous allocation of the resources we generate by iterative prioritization.

It is about people and their involvement in strategy making. An important priority is to reduce the distance between those devising strategy and those implementing that strategy – a gap I call the *air sandwich*. You can't be effective at executing strategy if the people devising the strategy *are like 10,000 feet from the ground*. They don't know about all the pot-holes and traffic lights. They don't understand the practical things people have to deal with in the execution of strategy. On the other hand, the people who have to execute the strategy don't have a broad vision or an understanding of the context, because they're stuck on the ground. They haven't taken part in the strategy making so they don't know the principles behind the decisions and the strategy itself. That's bad strategy making. It comes from the industrial and obsolete *Tayloristic* management division, blindly applied in today's highly-complex and high-variability contexts.

An adaptive company is one that is much more driven by principles rather than rules. The company's principles that everyone is expected to adhere to are about collaboration, conversation and co-creation. Another issue that must be confronted is the waste of talent. A static and hierarchical organizational design gives privilege and power to a few people who, by their nature, will try to preserve their position.

Stelio pointed out that this anarchic privilege applies even if it goes against the best interests of the organization, with the consequence that no space is made for young, talented people to be promoted.

Schuberg Philis – the Netherlands

This Dutch company, which provides mission-critical IT systems, has 280 employees and three co-founders. It has won an EU-OSHA award for Healthy Workplaces and Good Practice. My interviewee was Gerwin Schuring, one of the founders. He describes how the founding idea for the company came about by the founders asking themselves, 'What do we need to do to be a 100 per cent customer satisfaction company?' He added:

That is what inspires us. We like to get a pat on the back from a customer who says, 'That was a really good job'. We decided that we needed to focus only on the important stuff, we wanted to focus on mission-critical IT where the customer really cares. The stuff that matters to the company and to society. So, if we want to do that, why don't we totally shift the model and reject hierarchical structures? Just have really good people that are organized around the customer and who come up with a different type of decision-making. A team that aligns with the customer brings out that good stuff that you usually get when you are around the kitchen table with a good group of friends to plan a holiday trip or something. That is the kind of behaviour you would like to see in a company.

Building trust and having a big dream

Owing to their inherited ways of thinking and working, they found that every time they tried to remove rules some started creeping back in. So they introduced a discipline whereby every time the company reached the next growth step, they sought to remove rules. In one example, they scrapped the advanced system they had for tracking holidays and, instead, decided to trust each other to take about 25 days a year holiday. The company was highly ambitious from the start. It was a tiny start-up, competing against big players like IBM, HP and Microsoft, and it set out to win the top 25 customers in Holland, which was a huge challenge.

Involve customers in strategy development

They sought to build ambitious aims into the culture. The question the founders kept asking themselves was, 'What's next?' They discussed this throughout the whole organization and with their customers. Gerwin added:

> We organized a three-day summit and invited all our big customers. In the beginning it was a little bit awkward because they asked, 'Three days. What are we going to do?' We explained, 'Well, we're going to make a ten-year plan and we really would like your input.' Also, we felt that, because we were in our mid–40s and had a lot of kids, the question about purpose and legacy was something that we needed to address. So we organized this summit around, 'What does our purposeful future look like?'
>
> The cool thing was that when we asked everybody the question, 'What would you really like to do with the talent that we have as an organization?'

people came up with things that we wouldn't have dared say as management. [They] said that they want to save lives, they wanted to contribute to society and to help the poor. The three days were both emotional and transformational. It was a case of framing everyone's sense of purpose in their working lives in terms of how their work had meaning, how it made a contribution and how it left a legacy. It was at this summit that we decided to only work for purposeful clients.

He noted that this meant passing up on some business opportunities, but this was counter-balanced by maintaining motivation and a sense of purpose within the organization.

Get involved with communities and share knowledge

They also made a conscious decision to be open about their knowledge and to share their expertise for the benefit of communities. In the year before the summit, only a handful of colleagues gave talks at industry or community events. It is now common practice for any engineer or leader within Schuberg Philis to step forward onto a public forum or give an interview or write a blog:

We are now much more robust when it comes to innovation, because all these community influences now trickle into our organization. People just start using new technologies and experiment with them and, because we are not centralized anymore, we can have a situation where different people try to solve the same problem in two or three different places at the same time – and they come up with two or three different solutions.

In the old days we would have said, 'Oh we cannot have that, it's so inefficient', but now we see that it's great because people do it from their hearts and the best solution wins. Perhaps when room is made for two flavours, some people may prefer one flavour rather than the other. Why not?

We're pragmatic in our culture, we can say to each other, 'Hey guys, this doesn't make sense, we are now really doing three different things. Can we make up our minds on what we want and just agree on what the best option is?' Our culture permits us to say, 'This doesn't really add value to anyone, we can be much more efficient together.' That's something that should be instilled in the culture rather than in rules or processes.

The company values and nurtures long-term relationships with customers. Their first customers, as Gerwin notes, are still their customers, but they had to explain to their bosses why they were 'working with this quirky company'. While the emotional connection and a sense of social responsibility is important, the business sense in providing the service we do is central.

The impact of purposeful ways of working

The company generates a net profitability of about nine per cent in an industry where the average for the sector in the Netherlands is three per cent. For the eighth consecutive year Schuberg Philis obtained a 100% customer recommendation score with fifty per cent of these respondents being identified as *Superfans*, the highest percentage in the market. Gerwin observes, 'What happens with people who come work here [is that] it feels like coming home for a lot of people. A lot of people actually have invented this company in their heads already.' He acknowledges, however, that the highly participative style is not for everyone, 'because with this freedom also comes great responsibility'.

50 Key strategies for the *shift* in SMEs

SMEs are able to unleash their true entrepreneurial spirit and there are many examples of inspirational strategies used by SMEs to successfully humanize their organizations. Table 4.1 provides examples of the fifty key strategies that SMEs have used successfully.

TABLE 4.1 *50 key strategies for the shift in SMEs*

STRATEGY	CULTURE	RELATIONSHIPS	INDIVIDUALS	STRATEGY	SYSTEMS	RESOURCES
Hire on the basis of personality, character and cultural fit, not just on a CV	√		√	√		
Attract, hire and retain good quality staff	√		√	√		
Look after employees and they will look after the company (thank them for that)	√		√	√		
Follow values such as fun, wellbeing, creativity and adventure	√		√			
Live values and purpose at every opportunity until this becomes effortless			√			
Be yourself and act naturally in line with values that feel right, instead of obsessing with spreadsheets			√			
Relax and have more fun, then work becomes much less onerous and more innovation emerges with fewer hours put in			√			
Provide activities in the office that give a sense of wellbeing (e.g. yoga, pilates, meditation, etc.)	√			√	√	√

Provide a wellbeing fund for organizing anything that supports the wellbeing of employees			√	√
Use a *Dream Ball Machine* to make life better for employees (use it to make employees' dreams come true when a target is achieved)	√		√	√
Organize experiential dreams, brand launches and festival tours to promote the brand, network and have fun	√		√	√
Adopt an 'anything is possible' attitude. How we can live amazing fulfilled lives while changing this organization into a vehicle that enables the mindset, instead of a 'here is your job description' mindset	√	√		
Put faith and trust in your dreams		√	√	
Create a simple system for measuring the happiness of employees			√	√
Articulate what the company stands for in a simple way, and communicate that continuously			√	√
Find ways to measure intangibles such as relationships, wellbeing and creativity			√	√

(Continued)

TABLE 4.1 (*Continued*)

STRATEGY	CULTURE	RELATIONSHIPS	INDIVIDUALS	STRATEGY	SYSTEMS	RESOURCES
Form a community of other entrepreneurs, meet once a month and support each other				√	√	√
Use a points system instead of a hierarchical-based compensation system so anyone can earn more than the boss				√	√	
Use a transparent compensation system	√			√	√	
Use a flexible personal infrastructure so as to provide autonomy on how the work gets done				√	√	√
Integrate the company's commercial and social purpose	√			√		
Allow remote and flexible working patterns	√				√	
Provide clarity and purpose above making profit	√			√		
Create emotional engagement with the brand	√			√		
Create an environment that is a pleasure to work in	√				√	√

Remove divides between management and workers	✓			✓		
Provide share options for people who join		✓		✓		✓
Get the right people on board, trust them and treat them well	✓	✓		✓		✓
Rotate the CEO role		✓		✓		
Elect the board members by employees		✓		✓		
Interview people to ascertain their values and purpose	✓	✓		✓		
Use pivot points to manage distributed earnings		✓		✓		✓
Allow employees to managing their own time	✓	✓		✓		
Allow employees to have access to money for new initiatives		✓		✓		✓
Nurture transparency	✓	✓				
Allow tension and differences in opinion when they lead to collaboration and innovation		✓		✓		

(Continued)

TABLE 4.1 (*Continued*)

STRATEGY	CULTURE	RELATIONSHIPS	INDIVIDUALS	STRATEGY	SYSTEMS	RESOURCES
Assume that trust is given until it is lost	√		√	√		
Allow customers to get involved in governance	√			√	√	
Implement meritocracy. Adopt transparent and participative governance processes	√			√	√	
Assess contributions per task instead of assessing performance using a continuous flow of small feedback loops				√	√	
Allow decision making to be based on someone's involvement in governance	√			√	√	
Create a continuous flow of inclusive strategy making, where the distance between people deciding on strategy and implementing the same is minimal				√	√	
Use peer-based evaluation of contributions				√	√	
Implement collaborative decision-making processes				√	√	

Remove information processing bottlenecks. It is impossible for one person at the top of company to have the knowledge required to make all decisions	√	√			
Foster a culture of *inter-being*. An impact on one person can have start a chain reaction on others		√	√	√	√
Have a big dream and keep it alive			√		√
Involve customers in strategy development	√	√	√	√	√
Become part of a community's knowledge sharing		√		√	√
Develop long-term meaningful relationships with employees and customers		√	√	√	√

As with other sectors, the SME sector is unique in so many ways. Their strategies for humanizing their own organizations needs to be applied in their own specific context. This sector in particular provides opportunities for experimentation with new ideas and strategies – smaller organizations are easier to change and the benefits of any such changes tends to be more visible and will emerge more quickly.

 SEVEN REFLECTION POINTS FROM THIS CHAPTER

1 Do historical ways of working exist in your organization by reason of custom rather than because they serve the interests of the customer and the organization? For example, a high number of rules and strictly defined processes.

2 If you wish to move to a higher level of trust and engagement, do you have the mindset and commitment to do so?

3 Do you believe that moving towards a low-hierarchy, participative and informal model without the trust, communication and understanding to make it work may be counter-productive?

4 Do you see your company as being part of the wider community and the environment? Do you reflect on the nature of inter-dependence in a modern economy?

5 How do you deal with differences of opinion in your organization? Do you create space for honest discussion?

6 Do you focus on growth and monetary targets or do you see results as being a by-product of serving the customer well?

7 Do you honestly check the working experience for people in your organization so as to ensure that a healthy climate exists?

5

Humanized and humane: winning strategies from the non-profit sector

---

KEY INSIGHTS FROM THIS CHAPTER

- Many non-profit organizations lead the way in showing the effectiveness of Level 4 management.
- Increasing control and hierarchy can lead to higher costs and declining quality.
- The economy is not an entity separate from life. The same principles and ethical values apply both at work and at home.
- There are strong signs that the millennial generation will only accept an empowering leadership style.
- Command and control approaches can no longer cope with either complexity or rapid change. Bureaucratic, hierarchical organizations are no longer suited to the modern economy.

Serving society with engaged employees: non-profit sector challenges

Most non-profit organizations are set up with the core aim of improving society and the environment rather than making profits. Increasing concern over social inequality, the impact of regional conflicts, pollution and other environmental problems mean that activity in the non-profit sector remains high and the demands on many of these non-profit agencies are considerable.

However, having lofty aims does not guarantee an enlightened way of working and, while profit-maximization is never the aim, all organizations have to remain solvent in order to continue. This means that many of the organizational challenges facing non-profit entities are similar to those that face corporations: getting the right skills, teamwork, levels of motivation and creating a workplace structure designed to meet the needs of the organization – at a sustainable cost.

In my experience, you can find the same dehumanizing, dispiriting forms of management in the charitable sector as can be found in corporations, so humanizing the workplace is a challenge for all. The most proficient teams and organizations across the different sectors, private and non-profit alike, resemble one another quite closely. Their defining characteristics are the same at Level 4 or 5 in *The Management Shift*.

This chapter highlights some leading non-profit organizations that show us how to keep to the principles of Level 4 standards while simultaneously keeping costs under control. These inspirational and principled agencies illustrate some ingenious ways of helping to improve the quality of life while easing the suffering for those people for whom they have a duty of care.

Buurtzorg – the Netherlands

Jos de Block is CEO of Buurtzorg, a non-profit healthcare foundation based in the Netherlands that has 14,000 employees. He recalls that, as a nurse in the 1980s, he had experienced a Level 4 way of working in self-organized teams, but he later moved to larger organizations that had more hierarchy, more formal management systems and separate departments. While these hierarchical organizations appeared to be better organized, he observed that the quality of care had declined while costs had increased. So, in 2006 together with a group of friends, he sought to create a low-hierarchy, team-based way of working with a local focus. ('Buurt' means neighbourhood in Dutch.)

Growth though team networks of self-organizing nurses

He started with just one team in 2006, but within a few years the organization had grown rapidly and employed over 2,000 nurses:

> The nurses organized their own week. It was so easy for them. The nurses had a good relationship with the GPs, so they got referrals from them. They liked the fact that by organizing the work themselves they felt more responsible. It felt like they were free again. So, we are free to work according to our professional ethics, we don't have to follow orders from a strictly organized management and we can focus on the patient. We now support the needs of the patients and we can do what's necessary to deliver good care.

While they have had to introduce some back office functions, they kept the administration as light as possible and the number of rules as few as possible. Growth has been spectacular. Turnover rose from €1 million in 2007 to €12 million in 2008. At the time of this interview in 2017, turnover had increased to €400 million while the way of working has remained unchanged:

> With a different management approach we would never have achieved what we have now. If you want to make a transition, you can decide not to create

a command and control environment and, instead, focus on the self-support and self-management of the nurses. That's the way I've seen it.

Everybody benefits

From an organizational perspective, he calculated that their costs are twenty per cent lower than the average of other organizations. Further, their organization is more flexible and has the ability to adapt to changing circumstances. There are also huge savings for the government when it uses Buurtzorg, which, he says, delivers a better standard of care for the patients and more job satisfaction for the nurses themselves, who know they are trusted to do their job well and are in charge of the processes.

On Purpose – UK

On Purpose is a UK organization that seeks to integrate social, economic and environmental goals through the development of leaders. It is based on a critique of the way in which the economy has been perceived in recent decades, with corporates and profit-making organizations being seen as antithetical to social and environmental responsibility. As their website puts it, 'We're a community that helps find you work in the world, work that matters and work that you care about. We believe that only by doing this will we have a chance of solving society's most difficult problems.' Founder and Chief Executive Tom Rippin added:

> It doesn't make much sense to have one part of the economy predominantly creating profits while another part predominantly looks at the social or environmental aspects of things. They need to be combined and they need to be integrated, with trade-offs made more intelligently. For that to happen we believe we need leaders who understand both the social and the commercial worlds, people who can make those trade-offs and manage those kinds of organizations. Those are the leaders that we're trying to help develop through On Purpose.

Focus on and align individual and organizational purposes

A *shift* is needed at all levels: the level of the individual, the level of the organization and a shift at societal level. The *shift* should be based on a concept or purpose that is 'beyond yourself and beyond your family'. The organization should also be able to identify, articulate and act upon a purpose that is beyond the capabilities of its own shareholders and other interested parties. This implies a cultural *shift* towards understanding both the inter-dependence of society and our mutual reliance.

Tom often finds that the founding principles of many organizations are more enlightened than may be understood by the workforce, so they need to be rediscovered and reinvigorated:

These days, especially in very big companies, conversations are too focused on quarterly earnings, financial performance, shareholder value and all these kind of things, but if you go back to when these companies were founded they were founded with the objective of providing a service or product, and that is actually much more aligned with having a meaningful purpose.

One challenge is to find a way to create value and reward things that are related to purpose. Financial indicators such as profits and turnover tend to be used as a yardstick because they were easy to measure, but we need to think about how we can measure other, better things that are just as important, if not more important.

We need a paradigm shift and a systemic change

Such a cultural change cannot be enforced, he advises. Many changes must occur simultaneously: changes to systems and processes; changes to the culture and the way people talk about things; and changes in what people value. The difficulty faced is that people might give up on this because it seems too complex:

Even if we don't quite know how it's going to work, we have to try and do little things, keep on trying, keep on experimenting and see what works. We have to remember that the business system we currently have was created over the last 200 to 300 years and it is very sophisticated.

For example, systems of accounting have numerous built-in incentives that reinforce its structure. Ultimately, with the incoming of a new system some of those incentives will have to be changed, and that's not a simple thing. It's not something that can happen overnight, but it does need to start happening sooner rather than later.

What leaders need to do

On Purpose develops leaders who are willing to commit to a wider sense of social purpose, and Tom finds that much of the innovation is happening in the social enterprise world:

By exposing our leaders to that exciting and innovative space, we hope that they start picking up ideas and ways of doing things that contribute to and help, but eventually we hope they will help spread those ideas to more traditional companies.

But he sounded a warning:

We need to go through this *shift* for the right reasons. If you're doing it purely because you want your company to become more profitable, then you have the wrong mindset and I'm not sure you'll be able to achieve the *shift* in the first place, and I don't think it will be a very sustainable *shift*.

The Leadership Trust – UK

The Leadership Trust was founded in the UK in 1975 by David S. Gilbert-Smith and is based on the belief that better leadership is the route to a better society. Its charitable objectives are to advance the following:

1   Education and research in the fields of management and leadership, and the training of effective managers and leaders.

2   The education of the public, particularly in their knowledge and understanding of the principles of effective leadership.

3   The education of the public and, in particular, to encourage and support individuals who are, or wish to be, in a position of leadership and who wish to learn about and develop leadership skills.

It deploys research, thought leadership, influencing and training to achieve these objectives.

Winning hearts and minds to achieve a common purpose

The Trust's concept is that leadership is about winning over hearts and minds that are engaged around a common purpose, not simply issuing orders. 'You have to ignite that passion in people,' says Rob Noble:

> I think the common purpose, when it drifts from being a purpose that people just can buy into and get behind, i.e. the point at which it becomes a common purpose, people will support it, advocate it and tell others why it is incredibly important that you do what you do. That, for me, is the yardstick. That is the measure, because at that point they've probably developed a passion for the thing that you're trying to achieve. They have now bought into the purpose and they now support it emotionally. From that point you can then achieve amazing things.
>
> As much as people still hold the view that even the military is still very hierarchal and all about orders, that is only true in part. People have a brain, they have intellect and they have access to information that maybe they didn't have a hundred ago. They read newspapers, they listen to the news and they have a view.

Trying to motivate a group of people who have not bought into things politically is a real challenge. For me it was one of the reasons why I left the army. I was kept being told by senior officers and politicians that something was great, that it had to be done, that it was perfect, that it was wonderful and that we were doing it the right way. In reality, I could see the flaws in things. I think that as one becomes more senior it becomes even more difficult because you have got to try and advocate the wishes of other people.

People want more out of life now

Some people may be motivated by money, but not all, and the tendency may be diminishing:

> People will work for a certain organization if they are paid more money and the bonuses are bigger. It means that if they have a passion – for example if their passion is kite surfing and they want to go kite surfing more often in more exotic locations – then money alone may be a sufficient motivation for them to work really hard. However, I think that people want more out of life. I think those days of being solely motivated by money are an anachronism, if they haven't gone already.

A reduction in the level of bureaucracy is critical

A reduction in the number of tiers of management and in the level of bureaucracy is absolutely critical. The pace of change in society and the advances made in technology are such that organizations have to be much more responsive:

> Somehow the people on the factory floor, in sales offices or in hospital wards need to be able to interact with senior people so that strategic decisions are influenced by the real situation and its context.

Produce KPIs that go beyond just making money

The Leadership Trust is often asked to produce Key Performance Indicators (KPIs) that are not just financial. For example, KPIs can embrace sustainability, impact, gender and racial equality. Social media then increases the transparency of an organization's activities:

> You've got to be able to describe that you're moving the organization forward. That, for me, is critical. Organizations have got to move beyond paying lip service to, 'Oh yeah, we believe in diversity,' People are looking and people are scrutinising. Success comes through the people, or should come through the people. It cannot be effected through command and control. 'If you're achieving success through people, you'll achieve much more and you will be more resilient, and it doesn't take so much energy.'

The Drucker Institute – USA

The Drucker Institute is a social enterprise based in Claremont, California. Its mission is 'strengthening organizations to strengthen the society'.[1] Rick Wartzman is director of the KH Moon Center for a Functioning Society, an arm of the Drucker Institute. Wartzman, who served as the Institute's founding Executive Director, describes the tension that exists between efficiency and bringing out the most from people; between treating people almost as machines or giving them autonomy; between responsibility and a sense of dignity and fulfilment.

> I think there are particular pressures today that are working counter to the *shift*. The most insidious of all is this prevailing corporate ethos of maximising shareholder value. As the shareholder has become king, all other stakeholders, including workers, have seen their interests compromised. When that kind of system is in place managers and corporate

leaders do a lot of dumb things, things that endanger the health of their organization in the long-term, including failing to invest in people in the right way.

There are a lot of executives whose personal wealth is tied up with stock-based compensation who do everything they can to make profits rise in the short term. The most expedient way to do that is to cut costs. In turn, employees don't look like assets that should be invested in. They look like avoidable expenses. This is the major reason why job security has eroded, worker pay has stagnated for the past 40 years, benefits have declined and training for front-line employees has all but disappeared.

Keep the customer at the centre

Over the years, the Institute has consulted with executives at major companies to help them with innovation and with what Peter Drucker calls *planned abandonment*. That is, trying to figure out what needs to be stopped from being done so as to make room for new innovations. In its strategic advice it seeks to ensure that companies keep the customer at the centre. This involves much work on internal communications and trying to safeguard what Drucker called *information responsibility* – that is, making sure that information flows in the right form to the right place so that decisions can be made at a place close to the customer.

The shift is fundamental if organizations are to be sustainable

The Management Shift is fundamental to organizations that intend to be sustainable. Organizations that want to last for generations need to treat their workers well, to innovate continuously and be good members of the community. Wartzman advises, 'They need to provide a sense of purpose and really possess a sense of purpose. It must be genuine.' He encourages a sense of responsibility on the part of managers and leaders to employees:

Corporate leaders have a responsibility to their people that goes beyond sloganeering. Every executive will tell you, 'Our people are our most important asset,' but few act like it. Those [people] running companies need to remember that while they affect people's livelihoods and their ability to earn a decent wage, they also affect peoples' lives and their ability to live with fulfilment and dignity.

Developing people's skills, helping them to understand how their individual objectives feed into the overall mission of the organization and putting them in position to take advantage of their strengths, are not only the right things to do, they're very much in the interest of the enterprise itself.

Chartered Management Institute – UK

The Chartered Management Institute exists to professionalize the role of management within the UK economy. Many individuals are inadequately prepared for promotion to managerial positions, thus the CMI has created a structure of training and accreditation to equip people with the essential organizational and people-management skills required by the modern economy.

Command and control backfiring

Ann Francke is the chief executive of the CMI, having taken over the role following a successful career in corporate management. She recalls an incident from earlier in her career:

One day, I walked head down into the office, shut the door and they [my team] knocked on the door and said, 'can we speak with you?' They all came in and sat down. There were three of them and they said, 'you know, every day you come in, head down, straight into your office and you shut the door behind you. You never ask us how we are, you never say hello, you only bark orders and check on whether we've completed our tasks. That doesn't work for us. We need to be valued as people, so can you please change your behaviour?' I thought, 'Oh my goodness,' but they were absolutely right so I did change my behaviour. It was a wake-up call for me. I realized how important the people aspects are: valuing people, creating a culture of collaboration and trust and working together and sharing, but I hadn't created this.

Her style had been very much command and control, but she was made aware that it was backfiring. She changed her behaviour and adopted a more collaborative and inclusive style of management.

Flexible working patterns to suit individual needs

Key to this approach is recognizing that each person is different and has their own best way of working. This is to be compared to Level 3 ways of working that impose standard timetables and rules. A more engaging style involves flexibility and this extends to working hours:

> When I was a young mother I was divorced and it was very important to me that I took my daughter to school every day, but there were some very important management meetings that started at 9 o'clock and I would walk into those meetings at 9.30am, but I had a deal with my manager who said that was acceptable. Consequently, I extended that same right to flexible working to everyone who worked for me.

She found that such flexibility encourages diversity, with increased levels of diversity in the upper levels of leadership. Such a way of thinking also encourages a *higher ethic of care*, so that you care about your colleagues as people.

Valuing people and purpose

In common with other interviewees for this book, Ann detected a generational shift in attitude. People have become more vocal about matters such as diversity. She added:

I would like to think the same is true of the old-fashioned, rigid, testosterone fuelled [approach] that was all about power, money and corporate culture. I'd like to think that they are in existential decline because of the value *shift* that's happening in the world, and because the world's awareness of the need for this *shift* to happen. This is vital, and not least because of the financial crisis, because we're all so much more interconnected. As those [old] ways of working continue to decline, they are replaced by an increasing awareness of a new superior way of working, a way that values people, purpose and the better outcomes they can achieve. This will continue to advance.

In 2014 the CMI produced a report titled *Management 2020* in association with a parliamentary committee of the UK parliament. This report reiterated the three key principles of a well-led organization: purpose, people and potential. This reflected a similar conclusion to that found in the *Management Shift*. The results from a large-scale survey conducted as part of their research revealed that of some 2,000 organizations only forty-six per cent were very good when it came to purpose; just thirty-one per cent when it came to people; and only twenty-four per cent when it came to potential. With scores of below half, substantially below half on two of the principles, this demonstrated a seriously sub-optimal deployment of human capability.

This is not soft fuzzy stuff

The case for significantly improving the management of people is increasingly evidence-based and has become an economic necessity. She emphasized:

It isn't unproven speculation. It isn't soft fuzzy stuff. It's increasingly based on hard facts. The more that leaders at every level prioritise these things, talk about these things and demand these things both of themselves and others, the better off we'll be.

In common with other interviewees for this book, Ann points to the inefficiencies of the capital markets and the misguided focus on quarterly results:

It [the capital markets] focuses the minds of leaders and investors on short-term financial targets rather than underpinning the long-term systemic aspects of the *Management Shift*. When that happens we increasingly see organizations suddenly fall over, whether they're giant retailers like Tesco or the banks. Suddenly, you see that organizations that are relentlessly focused on meeting short-term targets and who ignore the underlying structure of their business find their objectives to be unsustainable.

Chartered Institute for Personnel Development – UK

The Chartered Institute for Personnel Development is the primary membership-based organization for personnel and human resource related professions in the UK. It has been established for over 100 years and has hubs in the UK, Ireland, the Middle East and Asia. It can confer a 'chartered status specialist' award in the field of human resources as well as in learning and development. The Institute also carries out independent research. Their Chief Executive, Peter Cheese, was interviewed for this book.

People are absolutely fundamental

Peter points to the paradox that trust in people management is declining just at the point that its importance is being better understood, so while this is an exciting time it is also challenging:

The workforce itself is changing. Younger people have a different expectation of work and I think they have a much higher expectation of what good leadership is about, and of being looked after. They're a little bit more socially aware in that regard. Then, of course, with technology and social media and everything else, things are so much more transparent.

Big contextual shifts

He highlighted some major contextual shifts: the nature of the workforce, the nature of how people want to work (with many wanting to work in small businesses), globalization and technology:

The leaders of the twentieth century were, by and large, not what you would call Level 4 leaders. They tended to be big ego, charismatic leaders who were more concerned about driving their own agenda. They took little interest in this more collective, more rational and more engaged kind of leadership that we talk about today.

I always say, don't confuse altruism with business. It's not just about being nice to people for the sake of being nice. This is about business. You have to look at things like sources of innovation. You have to look at things like organizations better reflecting the communities they serve. If I can't attract and retain all the people I need, how am I going to grow my business? If I can't create an environment that encourages diversity of thinking and diversity of inclusion, how am I going to innovate?

More broadly, how do I reflect better the societies and communities that I serve, which are equally important if I am to attract a much broader and diverse group of people into my business? In order to be innovative and stay viable, businesses have to be open and collaborative and work in a more networked way. Rigid hierarchies are a hindrance. This implies that we should create better leaders who are more attuned to working in a collaborative and engaging way. For all of those reasons, a *shift* from Level 3 to Level 4 has become a real business priority.

The importance of culture and purpose

This is a cultural challenge that has to be led from the top and should be based on identifying and setting strong values with a strong sense of purpose. Leaders have to possess more than technical qualifications, they have to live the values of this strong culture.

For the most part, when you say we're doing leadership development it's about big strategy, financial scenario planning and all those other good things that are important, but very little is said about the essential elements of leadership. I think it's a lot to do with the legacy: what we valued, what we felt was important and what was on the business agenda. Then you go back to that old mantra, which again is part of the legacy, that what can be measured gets done. If I can't measure it, then I can't touch it.

What does HR as a profession need to do?

He acknowledges that the HR profession itself has been too inward looking. It has to be prepared to challenge what has been done in the past. For example, the profession should reflect the findings on neuroscience, behavioural science, behavioural economics and positive psychology, and then incorporate an understanding of the importance of values, ethics and trust. This challenges what he calls *legacy management thinking*:

If you think that shouting at people is the way to get people to work better, to be more engaged, to be more effective and to learn, then here's all the science that completely contradicts you. We've got to get better at management, get better at the data and get better at analytics. We must extract data in order to inform strategic thinking and management behaviour.

Roffey Park – UK

Roffey Park is a highly regarded executive education and research organization that was set up in 1946 and is currently based in West Sussex. It is dedicated to developing learning approaches that enable individuals to reach their full potential, both at work and in their personal lives. It offers a range of courses, undertakes research and produces publications from its bases in England and Asia, the latter being based in Singapore.

Offer power to other people

Michael Jenkins, the Chief Executive, has sought to devolve power since taking over the role in 2009, having noted that a significant amount of power was vested in the position of CEO. In doing so, he sought to draw upon one of the organization's great strengths, its strong sense of purpose to help people achieve and give of their best. He has overseen a diminution of formal hierarchy and encouraged a more collective form of leadership, including the launch of multi-disciplinary cluster groups [that break down 'silos'].

Build the culture around self-management

We have a culture that is very much built around self-management so our pedagogical philosophy is very much about inviting participants onto our programmes and for them then to take ownership of their learning. This is the way we live and work at Roffey Park. It is about people having a strong sense of self-management and, within our faculty body, that is something that people prize.

Deciding with them what the challenges are going to be and then getting to work on tackling those challenges is the way that I generally like to work, but what I have learned over the years is that not everybody shares the same approach and attitude to their work. There are, understandably, colleagues who are less comfortable with ambiguity and who feel much more comfortable with the setting of very clear parameters within which they are then required to work. They prefer to have a very solid view of what their goals and objectives are.

VUCA has always been with us

In common with other interviewees, Michael describes a world that is Volatile, Uncertain, Complex and Ambiguous (VUCA), but points out that this has always been the case:

> I think that organizations that can make the *shift*, that you have so brilliantly described, are the ones that can survive in a world, which in my opinion has always been uncertain. When we look at the world around us I would concede that uncertainty is probably increasing apace right now. Therefore, it is really important to revisit the question of our purpose and ask the question once again, 'Do we know why we are here, doing what we are doing? Is what we are doing still appropriate to and suitable for the people we are supposed to be serving?'

Communication is critical

One lesson for all leaders is that the messages you communicate in a particular way will be received and understood by different people in different ways. This means that communication has to be continuous and that leaders must continually check their own understanding. They must also check how people feel about what they are doing as well as how they understand things that matter to them. Flexibility is vital, as strategies often have to be adjusted in this volatile world.

Go slow to go fast for long term benefits

The communication challenge is best understood as a paradox – go slow to move fast. What this means is that making the effort to be consultative saves time by keeping people informed and on board. You can then build a shared understanding of the direction of travel:

> I have always felt that the maxim *go slow to go fast* is a very valuable and it is one of many lessons I have learnt over the years. Establishing foundations

and taking care over how you set something up can reap real benefits in the long term.

You must have the forbearance to withstand and be strong in the face of people who pressurise you to move faster – that is important if you want to *go slow to go fast*. You have to balance that maxim so as to be in tune with market needs and market changes. You can then change the direction of the organization accordingly.

Create compassionate workplaces

Michael says that we should not be afraid to talk about creating warmer relationships in the workplace and further says that we must encourage compassion, thoughtfulness and consideration of others:

Not just because we spend so much of our time at work, but because I think that there is also a business imperative as well. We need to look at compassion not as something that is pink and fluffy, but as something that is a key ingredient in involving the engagement of the people who work for the organization. It is through building that engagement that we can start to see some tangible outcomes in terms of improved productivity.

His final piece of advice on people making the *Management Shift* is, 'Don't wait, but at the same time don't rush. Go slow in order to go fast, and don't assume that there is ever a final destination.'

The Drucker Society Europe – Austria

The Drucker Society Europe, in keeping with the Drucker Institute based in the USA (featured earlier in this chapter), is dedicated to facilitating ongoing dialogue between management practitioners, academics and other interested parties with the object of encouraging innovation in line with

Peter Drucker's enlightened philosophy. At a practical level, this means influencing behaviours and attitudes while encouraging sound management practices. Particular priorities for the European Society are to:

1   Promote management as a vital organ of a functioning society.

2   Identify and close the responsibility gap and address the ethical challenges of business.

3   Encourage knowledge work and knowledge worker productivity.

4   Encourage an entrepreneurial society.

5   Drive innovation in the twenty-first century.

6   Motivate the younger generation, with a view to sustaining the legacy of the Drucker ideals.

Change the context of how a business is run to change managerial behaviour

Richard Straub is President of the Drucker Society Europe and founder of the Global Peter Drucker Forum. He points to the contrast between a widespread acknowledgement of the flaws in organizational management practices and the slowness of progress in many organizations:

> The challenge we are all facing is why is this taking such a long time? Why are there so few model cases? Why is it that employees are still far from being able to use their potential in companies? There's a huge discrepancy between what we should have achieved and what we actually have. That's one of these challenges and I think there is no simple answer.
>
> I certainly think that there has not been a sufficient appreciation of the way management works in large scale environments. You cannot solve the issue by simply telling managers to change the way they operate; you must also change the context for them.

Peter pointed out that this goes beyond individual managers, companies and leaders, especially if they are under pressure to increase shareholder value in the short term:

Many managers are very reasonable people who try to do reasonable things, but I think what has not changed, or what has changed in the wrong direction, is the framework and context in which managers operate. That's part of Wall Street and the stock markets: how they measure, how they invest and, behind that, what do the investors require?

The management practices today are worse than twenty years ago

The distorting effect of such pressures from the investment community has actually produced management practices that have deteriorated over the past two decades. He concluded:

What can the managers do? Yes, some will try to swim against the tide, but I think, unfortunately, it's limited to the few outstanding or extraordinary personalities who lead their companies, because without the leadership you can never get there.

If the leadership does not support these changes, it will be very difficult for middle management to make these changes work at their level.

Foster entrepreneurial spirit

Those organizations that do take a lead to become more sustainable are characterized by the way in which they innovate and maintain that entrepreneurial spirit. This spirit is easy to lose in larger organizations that behave like machines, who, in some cases, [only] retain an entrepreneurial edge by buying start-ups. However, the healthiest and most resilient larger organizations nurture an entrepreneurial spirit throughout the business. That's what should happen and that's the biggest challenge that we face.

Business as a force of good for society

A central quest of the Drucker Society is to instil an understanding in managers that they are a part of society, not just business engineers. This can be a considerable challenge when it comes to competitive and cost pressures, but it is the way to create better long-term value. 'Managers must develop their own standing and their own strength as a professional group, who can and do articulate what's right and what's wrong.'

The National Centre for Strategic Leadership – UK

More than twenty organizations joined together to establish the National Centre for Strategic Leadership, a UK organization dedicated to the vocational development of managers and leaders at all levels within the economy – including members of the C-Suite. Founder organizations include leading universities, colleges and coaching specialists. In 2014 it became part of The Babington Group of training and education providers.

People are the ones that generate the money

Nigel Girling was the founding Chief Executive. He described a problem of an economy that was over-managed but under-led. This is an indicator of a bureaucratic Level 3 practice that pays insufficient attention to the people who ultimately create all the value, and to the fact that organizations exist to create value in ways that go beyond the financial:

My kind of approach has always been about how we make this a joyful experience for everybody who has anything to do with it: employees, suppliers and customers. How do we make this something that is human and adds value to the human experience?

We've spent the last three decades trying to train first-line managers and supervisors as well as new people coming into this, but we still haven't affected the mindsets of those people who dictate how everything works. New people come in with lots of ideas, but they eventually get assimilated and absorbed into the old way of doing things, then off we go commanding and controlling again.

We need to shift it quick

To counter the prevailing culture is a huge challenge, but it is one that has to be undertaken. I think we need to *shift* it [the culture] quick because I think there's all kinds of ramifications if we don't. One of the things we need to do, I think, is to stop promoting psychopaths and start promoting people! Look at the rubble of the economic meltdown that we've only just climbed out of. A lot of that was brought about by that style of leadership.

Simple disciplines such as promoting the right people who will then develop others rather than promoting those who take a more exploitative approach will help rectify this, but he acknowledges that the track record on this needs to improve markedly:

If you want innovation you've got to have people who are engaged enough, committed enough and care enough to want to come up with great ideas. Then you must enable them to do something about it. You can't do that in a kind of vertical, horizontal matrix. You've got to do it in an organization that creates space, and organizations only create space if someone important thinks it matters.

Business schools and government should champion the shift

Business schools need to reform themselves radically, he argues:

They have been factories that churn out MBA robots that go and run companies with spreadsheets. Instead, they should increase the leadership content of MBAs to make them much more people-focused.

I also think that the government has a huge part to play in all of this. Employers need to demand a different type of leader and create a different type of dynamic to support and promote differently. The government needs to fund that and support it in some way. Give people the opportunity.

Turkeys don't beg for Christmas

One of the problems with the modern economy, which he argues is dysfunctional and too focused on finance and on short-term indicators, is that there is insufficient accountability. After the financial crash too many of those institutions responsible for bringing about this crisis were able to retain their profits. As Nigel put it, 'Turkeys don't beg for Christmas.' He argued that many [companies] became discredited along the way, with the result that many of the more talented, younger people no longer wished to work in the speculative part of the market economy. They want to do something worthwhile:

> I think that the bigger organizations are already starting to see that just having a salary and prospects is no longer sufficient to attract the best people. If we don't pick up on that, that wave is going to pass them by and it'll roll over the top of them. I think a lot of our biggest organizations are going to find themselves in a lot of difficulty in ten years or twenty years' time. Maybe not tomorrow, but soon enough.

The McLeod Report for Engagement[2] estimates that it is costing UK businesses around £30 billion a year not to have fully engaged people, and only about thirty per cent of employees are actively engaged in the work they do:

I wouldn't be surprised if you're talking twenty per cent, thirty per cent of turnover in those organizations, minimum. In some less profitable organizations, this is the difference between survival and prosperity.

Adding value to the human experience

Radical change starts with people inside thinking, 'What is the point and the value of what you do as a leader?' If you cannot describe a socially valid purpose in human terms, then the organization is not doing anything useful. If all you're there to do is to look important and trouser the money, that's not much different to being a drugs dealer or an arms runner or anything else. There is no human value. So how are you adding value to the human experience?

Institute for Leadership and Management – UK

The Institute for Leadership and Management is a professional body with more than 30,000 members. It is dedicated to encouraging great leadership in all walks of life and all sectors of the economy. It seeks to instil values of leadership conduct that is ethical as well as visionary and innovative.

There is a strong connection between poor management and unhappy people

Charles Elvin, the Chief Executive at the time of this interview, acknowledged that the general standard of management and leadership should be much higher and he challenged the notion that conduct and values at work should be judged differently from other settings:

There is a very strong connection between poor management, lousy leadership and unhappy people. You can make everyone a lot happier by making their manager better at their role, with the result that the people they manage and lead generally have a better time at work. Work and life, companies and your life, aren't separate. They're all part of the existence we live in.

The idea that the ethics and values we hold at work are different from ethics and values we hold at home is nonsense. I think the [management] *shift* is highly desirable. I think it's possible for certain individuals and certain organizations to do it and, over the longer term, they will do it better. This shouldn't imply a utopian dream where everyone's a concert pianist, it is more about seeking an upward *shift* in purpose and motivation that will help the company as well as the individuals.

We need a high level of self-awareness to shift

He observed that, while technology has advanced rapidly over the last 100 years, research into human psychology has remained unaltered. There is a need to increase the rate at which we learn from findings on psychology: from research such as the importance of emotional intelligence and, especially, dimensions of self-awareness. That is to say, an understanding of yourself as well as others, how you interact with your environment and the consequence of those interactions:

First of all, the individual must have a level of ability to see and care about it. Secondly they need to have seen that this has an impact, or they have had it done to them (so they have some sort of direct experience). We all know the way bad managers are, but we're really bad at spotting good ones. You know, because they just happen and you think, 'Oh'. Then you reflect back after a few days and think, 'They were really good because they didn't create perfection and because they didn't create issues.' You believe you've done it yourself.

You remember that famous quote about leadership, 'You don't think about the person who sort of quietly and gently allowed you, led you, corralled you, and suggested all those things that got you there.'

The danger of a 'I can't get any better' CEO's mindset

The best leaders remain humble, he argued. A real warning sign for a chief executive is when they have had a run of success and they believe that, 'I can't get any better.' He added:

> They start to believe they're infallible. They start to believe they're the Pope. You know, they start to live in this world where they've surrounded themselves increasingly with people that reinforce that view, and when someone becomes very senior they stop wanting the challenge, or frequently do. I think this is the biggest challenge in a *start from the top* approach. Yes, I totally agree there is no question that the culture and the environment of an organization is driven very much by the [culture] that is set from the very top, but that person at the very top has to want all the consequences, and the biggest barrier is his ego.

Trust is like a diamond

He argues that trust is measurable and definable, but it's also like a diamond. It is incredibly strong in one direction, but with one tap it can shatter. Even in benign circumstances, it can be more brittle than it appears:

> Trust is a personal relationship. It's an emotion. People talk about trust as something outside. It's not. Trust is your relationship with a person. If you trust someone things happen so much more easily, and better. It's a wonderful corporate oil, but it's the reverse if you don't have it. Everything jams up.

You cannot manage complexity through micromanagement

'You cannot manage complexity through micromanagement and control,' he finds. This is counter-intuitive to many, but the way to manage complexity is to empower and trust people while reducing your own direct control. No manager can have all the knowledge, and they can be subject to information overload with social media and incoming emails:

> You then have different languages, different cultures, different countries and different legislations. I mean, what we're expecting managers to deal with is staggering. You can't be in it all. You have to move away and trust other people, which then gives room for leadership.

50 key strategies for the *shift* in non-profit organisations

Non-profit organizations have made a hugely positive impact on society for centuries. They helped abolish slavery, created advances in health and medicine, alleviated poverty and protected the environment. They have inspired many people around the world to give of their best and have improved the quality of life for those around them. Their campaigns are often inspirational, and many of them use inspirational, humane strategies. Table 5.1 provides examples of the fifty key strategies that these non-profit organizations have successfully used to do good for society. As with other sectors, the non-profit sector is unique in many ways, therefore strategies for humanizing non-profit organizations need to be applied within their own specific context.

TABLE 5.1 *50 key strategies for the shift in non-profit organizations*

STRATEGY	CULTURE	RELATIONSHIPS	INDIVIDUALS	STRATEGY	SYSTEMS	RESOURCES
Allow self-organization	√			√		
Foster individual responsibility at work	√		√			
Encourage freedom to organize work according to professional ethics, not strict rules	√		√			
Utilize the power of team network	√	√				
Encourage transparency in all activities	√	√	√	√		
Expect accountability through giving responsibility	√	√	√			
Focus on self-support	√		√			
Use the same principles to scale up the system at different locations				√	√	
Use simplicity in operations				√	√	
Express purpose beyond yourself and your family	√		√			
Articulate and act on a purpose that is beyond your own organization and shareholders	√		√	√		

(Continued)

TABLE 5.1 (*Continued*)

STRATEGY	CULTURE	RELATIONSHIPS	INDIVIDUALS	STRATEGY	SYSTEMS	RESOURCES
Identify passionate champions to drive the shift		√	√			
Measure, value and ultimately reward the things that are related to purpose	√			√	√	√
Measure, value and ultimately reward the things that are related to societal impact	√			√	√	√
Measure, value and ultimately reward the things that are related to environmental impact	√			√	√	√
Do small things and small experiments to see what works				√	√	
Start doing things in new ways that focus on financial sustainability as well as societal impact				√	√	
Focus on winning both the hearts and minds of employees	√			√		
Ignite passion in people around a common purpose			√	√		
Reduce the level of bureaucracy					√	

Reduce the number of middle managers. Improve communication	✓				
Produce KPIs that go beyond just making money	✓	✓			
Focus on corporate communications and integrity		✓		✓	✓
Understand that success comes from people		✓	✓		✓
Use role models to lead by example		✓	✓	✓	✓
Keep the customer at the centre		✓			✓
Ensure that information flows in the right form and in the right place	✓	✓			
Enable those who are closest to the customer to make decisions	✓	✓			✓
Provide employee development, fulfillment and a sense of responsibility	✓	✓			✓
Foster autonomy and accountability among employees	✓	✓	✓		✓
Show potential employees that you really want them to join. Call them	✓	✓			✓

(Continued)

TABLE 5.1 (*Continued*)

STRATEGY	CULTURE	RELATIONSHIPS	INDIVIDUALS	STRATEGY	SYSTEMS	RESOURCES
Adopt a collaborative and inclusive management style	✓		✓	✓		
Allow flexible working patterns that suit individual needs	✓		✓	✓	✓	
Understand that people are not a cost, they are assets	✓		✓	✓		
Reward CEOs on how they deliver purpose				✓	✓	
Embrace principles about purpose, people and potential	✓			✓		
Run companies like employee-owned mutuals				✓	✓	✓
Recruit and promote people who reflect the values of leadership	✓			✓	✓	
Offer power to other people in your organization	✓		✓	✓		
Build culture around self-management	✓		✓	✓	✓	
CEOs must provide advice, support, guidance and counseling			✓	✓		

Revisit the purpose and ask, 'do we know what we are doing why we are doing it?'		√			√
Adjust strategy along the way in terms of when new information becomes available		√			√
Create space for innovation	√		√	√	√
Change the context of how the business is to be run in order to change managerial behaviour	√		√		√
Foster entrepreneurial spirit	√				√
Move emphasis away from short-term targets toward achieving long-term objectives			√		√
Create a management culture where managers understand they are part of society	√	√			
Create an organizational context that is built on trust	√	√	√		√
Promote people-focused people	√		√		

SEVEN REFLECTION POINTS FROM THIS CHAPTER

1 Does your management make improving working conditions for their staff a priority?
2 Do you tend to assume that humanitarian aims are enough in themselves, or do you make a conscious effort to implement the principles of *The Management Shift*?
3 If you work in a non-profit, campaigning organization, do you challenge short-termism and greed, greed that can distort the economy both internally and externally?
4 A move towards *The Management Shift* would have a significant positive impact on economic value creation. Do you make the economic and business case as well as the social and environmental case?
5 In moving toward a Level 4 workplace, does change start with the most senior executives?
6 Hubris and arrogance are common pitfalls for senior executives, e.g. the belief that 'I can't get any better'. What measures has your organization put in place to ensure accountability and managerial development at all levels?
7 Command and control can be features in the non-profit sector. Are you moving toward the creation of self-empowered teams?

PART III

HOW TO LEVERAGE HUMANE CAPITAL IN YOUR ORGANIZATION AND TRANSFORM WORKPLACE PERFORMANCE AND PROFIT

6

What the evidence tells us: Data patterns from interviewees show how the best-led organizations succeed

KEY INSIGHTS FROM THIS CHAPTER

- Evidence for high-performance, healthy workplaces are now well established. They are no longer anecdotal, nor are they a correlation.
- There are proven, established ways to move towards a higher level of operating while humanizing conditions.
- The best approaches should be made at the individual, team and organizational level.
- There are eight key pillars for leveraging *humane capital*.
- Change is more sustainable if is linked to systems and processes and not reliant upon a single leader.

Research evidence from this study

Chapters 2, 3, 4 and 5 presented examples of case studies on humanizing organizations in corporations, the public sector, SMEs and the non-profit sector. Specific strategies for creating and leveraging humane capital in these sectors were presented by leaders in these sectors, which can be used in the context of a specific sector. These strategies emerged from the analysis of the qualitative data that was made available from interview transcripts that extended to more than 272,000 words in total.

I am aware that, superficially, the evidence that superior business performance at Level 4 and 5 workplaces may appear to be correlative or anecdotal. Therefore, I made a conscious choice in this book to select diverse case studies, to address concerns that what may work in one sector or type of organization may not work in another, and to demonstrate that the principles are universal. Yet, and quite understandably, some managers, business owners, advisers and others ask for a more rigorous analysis.

This chapter presents research evidence from the data obtained from fifty-eight leaders who were interviewed for this project. Appendix 1 shows core interview questions. Appendix 2 shows a list of all the interviewees and their affiliations at the time of interview, the themes covered in the interview and their industry sector. Appendix 3 provides some analysis of demographic data related to the interviewees and their organizations.

All interview transcripts were analysed manually and by qualitative data analysis software (NVivo, version 11.4.0). The data in these transcripts was coded against the broad themes covered by the interview questions as well as against the key constructs of the *6 Box Leadership Model*.[1] The latter was chosen as the framework for data analysis because of its intensive research background. Some of the data patterns discovered from this analysis are presented both in this chapter and in Chapter 7 – this includes data obtained from the manual thematic analysis of all transcripts. Appendix 4 provides further information about research methodology and the data analysis used in this project.

The patterns that emerge from these analyses are strong and consistent, giving a clear direction as regards to the key elements of leveraging *humane capital* and creating a high-performance workplace. One conclusion is that change has to start with the individual, so before presenting the analysis I will present two more personal stories that illustrate this.

Patterns of data: the emerging truths of combining humane leadership with better results

The Big Shift starts with individual shift

The journey towards the *Big Shift* from Level 3 to Level 4 starts with the mindset of the individual and then spreads like a ripple affecting people around them, eventually affecting the entire organization. One of the interviewees in this project, Chris Stern, a former General Manager with Scandinavian Airlines, shared an inspirational story about his own individual *shift*. Chris left his corporate life and spent time finding his own purpose, he re-evaluated his lifestyle and he is now a successful board adviser and coach for executives. He shared his thoughts on how his own organization went from a Level 4 to a Level 3 leadership. Just as he was becoming convinced of the merits of enlightened leadership, his own management team required him to obey more rules and he became boxed in. He said:

> I could feel that there's something going on in the world out there and I wanted to be a part of it, but I really didn't know how. I didn't know how to navigate in it, I didn't know how to make sense of it and I didn't know what my role was. It was easy to go back to the world I knew and hide, but at some point I knew that this was not sustainable. It just wasn't right anymore because the company and I were diverging.

He reached the conclusion that finding purpose and operating at Level 4 was of overriding importance, more so than his own short-term career prospects. This was the moment when Chris started his own individual *shift*, and now has a very different, happier, fulfilling life:

> The majority of people I meet in my professional and personal network say they that they do not like their job or that they do not like their boss or they are too stressed. I'm thinking, 'Why would I join that again, when I have an opportunity to do something else?'

In order to go through this individual *shift*, he recommends that we start by removing ourselves from toxic environments. This may be more difficult for some rather than others, but he warns of the dangers of staying in an unpleasant working environment for extended periods of time. He uses the parable of the boiling frog. The premise is that if a frog is placed in boiling water it will immediately jump out, but if it is placed in cold water that is slowly heated it will not perceive the danger until it is too late, and by then it will have been cooked to death:

> I think a lot of people are no longer in Level 2 or Level 1 organizations because most people would just get out of there. I think they're mostly in a Level 3 environment and it's like boiling the frog. It's not that bad, but it ain't good enough.

He simplified his life by reducing the number of assets he owned and by eliminating personal debt. He rents an apartment, shares a car and cycles as much as possible. He finds it liberating and it gives him peace of mind. While he acknowledges that everyone's situation is different, he points to the personal benefits of creating an economic environment that allows individuals the time to work on their own personal transition. It is a very different way of looking at life:

You've got to take the personal *shift* to reboot yourself and I don't know, but for me it was looking at personal values and understanding what was going on in this *VUCA* world. The results may be different for different people, but all I see now are opportunities, and though things can take me in many different ways I feel I'm on the right path. I also feel so fortunate. After I made this *shift*, this *mind shift*, the type of people that I now meet are different. I attract different people, I connect with different people.

The power of the individual *shift* and the power of mind is well known to Justin Packshaw, an adventurer, entrepreneur and philanthropist with a military background. He also represented Britain at sailing in the Whitbread Round the World Race, as well as leading expeditions to the north and south poles and summiting Mount Everest:

The superb training one gets in the Army teaches you to think with clarity, to be open-minded, logical and extremely people driven. Obviously that system teaches individuals to make decisions about the most important commodity that there is, which is life. Good judgement is imperative.

Between serving in the Army and leading expeditions I have learned that the most effective way to get the best out of people is to have a very clear goal, something that everyone in your team buys into and understands. This is imperative if you are stepping into the unknown and you are doing something you know will stretch you and push you to the point of exhaustion. All of this has been a brilliant bedrock for teaching me life skills and the power of *belief*.

This perspective prompted a reflection on how to bring the best out of yourself and other people and teams in a generic way. A way that applies to all organizations, that is based around the core principle of treating people well, and making them feel important, involved and listened to.

Your *shift*, from an apathetic organization to one that is more collaborative, is imperative. We have to encourage companies to be more forward-looking and to have an attitude that they can do even more. Moving from Level 3 to Level 4 is an evolution. It is also a work in progress that involves changes in behaviour that lead to changes in practice, rather than a wholesale break with old ways. It's about trusting individuals, empowering them to be their best and making them feel part of a conscientious family. This creates a happy workforce who enjoy coming to work and are loyal.

Because of the innate and obvious risks, his experience of leading expeditions highlights this more clearly than any other context. The team and its leaders have to be simultaneously responsive, forward-looking and capable of building a tight unit. They need to be aware of the team's strengths and weaknesses. It's not a case of, 'I want to know your weaknesses so that I can exploit them,' he says. Rather it's, 'I want to know your weaknesses because I want to protect you.' Success means relying on everyone:

> It's about allowing those individuals and the autonomous teams that work within the organization to have a shared purpose and a commitment and a desire to create a thorough and direct form of communication. It is not about holding people up or restricting them. It is about everyone feeling that they are an important and integral part of the organization.
>
> Trust is a big part of this. This creates the space to allow people's skills to come to the surface and to be used. It fuels confidence, loyalty and excitement, and it gives individuals a position of value and importance. As individuals and organizations, it is important that we just keep pushing and moving towards unbounded growth – your own Level 4. We are becoming a people-driven society and you need to think big if you are to challenge assumptions and achieve what's possible. My final thought, 'I think we all just need to be braver!'

Patterns of data on the individual shift from NVivo analysis

Parts of the interview transcripts that relate to the *individual shift* were analyzed using NVivo software in the context of the key factors within the 6 Box Leadership Model. Table 6.1 shows the top eight factors influencing the *shift* in an individual mindset, as well as their frequency. That is, the number of responses where a particular theme was mentioned during interviews about the *individual shift*.

For example, mindset and attitude are the key drivers for going through the *shift*, followed by motivation (linked to the mindset), alignment of individual and organizational values (discrepancy in these values would hinder the *shift*) and a sense of purpose and passion for work.

Emotional intelligence, i.e. having an awareness of one's own feelings and those of others, helps the *individual shift*. Opportunities for learning and development available within an organization also foster the *shift*, as do good interpersonal skills and the self-organization of employees in communities where they can collaborate and help each other anchor new behaviours.

TABLE 6.1 *Top eight themes related to the individual* **shift**

Theme	Frequency
1. Mindset and attitude	20
2. Personal motivation	9
3. Alignment of individual and organizational values	8
4. Sense of purpose and passion for work	7
5. Emotional intelligence	4
6. Opportunities for learning and development	3
7. Interpersonal skills	3
8. Self-organization of employees in communities	3

The eight pillars of leveraging *Humane Capital* in organizations

The NVivo analysis of all data transcripts identified the eight key themes that drive the *shift* in organizations. They relate to the *how* of the *Big Shift* towards becoming a more humane organization, and they show the key areas that each organization needs to focus on in order to do good and to do well at the same time.

Figure 6.1 shows a high-level summary of the top eight pillars of the *Big Shift* towards leveraging *humane capital* in organizations. Table 6.2 provides further insight into these key themes, including their frequency of occurrence when these themes were mentioned in interviews as drivers of the *Big Shift*,

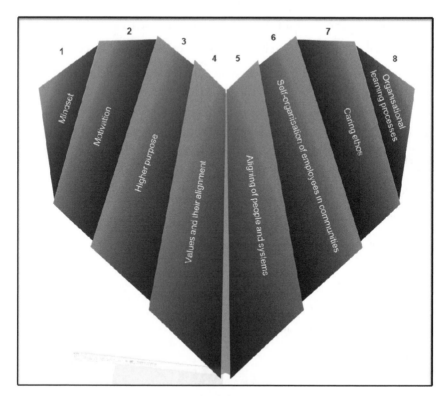

FIGURE 6.1 *The 8 pillars of Humane Capital.*

TABLE 6.2 *The eight pillars of Humane Capital, frequency of themes and key area*

Top eight themes	Frequency	People / Process Area
1. Mindset	88	*People*
2. Motivation	46	*People*
3. Higher purpose	37	*People*
4. Values and their alignment	36	*People*
5. Alignment of people and systems	33	*People* and Process
6. Self-organization of employees in communities	33	*People* and Process
7. Caring ethos	30	*People*
8. Organizational learning processes	30	*People* and Process

together with an indication of whether they come from the *People* or *Process* areas of the 6 Box Leadership Model.

Data in the above table show that all eight top themes are either focused on *People* or *People and Process* areas. This provides compelling evidence on the importance of focusing on people in order to create high-performing, highly-profitable, highly-engaging and purposeful organizations. Each of these themes is further described in subsequent sections, including representative quotes from some of the interviewees.

1. Mindset: Changing the mindset of leaders and employees

These findings fundamentally challenge the Level 3 approach, which is dominated by fine-tuning structures and reporting lines, while expecting people to slot into the corporate machine. What the evidence tells us is that, ultimately, the business relies on teams of people and that the structure ought to support them, rather than the other way around. Positive change starts, but does not stop, at the individual level. Many of the world's leading organizational and management thinkers interviewed for this book arrived at the same conclusion. Jules Goddard, Fellow at the London Business School, observed:

> If the economic model of rational decision making continues to be followed, we will stay in rigidly hierarchical and bureaucratic organizations of inertia. Escaping these counter-productive structures and habits requires inspiration, emotion, courage, and even love. It needs a different kind of human relationship. Those virtues are not something the economic model of rationality helps us with.

Marshall Goldsmith, one of the most influential business thinkers and executive coaches in the world, has helped many leaders to go through a *shift* in mindset. They (the leaders) achieved positive long-term changes in behaviour for themselves, their people and their teams:

> The key variable for our success is not me, it's the people I work with. They are all dedicated and want to make a positive difference. Those are the kind of people that are willing to make the *shift* you talk about. Their only question is, 'how can I best do this?', not 'should I do this?'

He encourages leaders to get into the habit of asking for input. They then get confidential feedback in terms of how they're viewed by their colleagues. They can then select important behaviours that need to be improved and then develop a follow-up system to measure these behaviours and their impact. He added:

> A lot of research shows that if leaders increase effectiveness, it's perceived by everyone around them. There is a high correlation between positive change and employee engagement, and a high correlation between positive change and the overall effectiveness for the organization. My advice is not to just simply understand this in an abstract intellectual form, but to get feedback that effects behavioural change in a way that is consistent with the change the leaders want to make. This isn't an intellectual exercise, this is an exercise in real behavioural change.

The importance of the mindset of leaders is emphasised by Rob Wirszycz, a former Director General of the UK IT Trade Association, now known as TechUK. 'Most organizations are influenced by the person who is at the top, very heavily influenced.' He shared an example of the CEO he worked with:

He would stop people doing their normal work. Nothing could be done without him knowing or without him having an opinion on it. It became a bit of a nightmare. It was almost like being in a family where one of the parents is an alcoholic or has some such problem, and the kids kind of worked around it. What people were doing was working around him and finding strategies to work around this dysfunctionality.

The importance of a leader's mindset is echoed by Richard Barrett, Chairman of Barrett's Values Centre:

It all begins with the leadership because the culture in the organization is a reflection of the leadership consciousness, thus the culture looks like a mirror image of the leader. You can't achieve a cultural transformation without first transforming the leaders.

In the relatively benign situation where leaders are already operating at a higher level of consciousness, but haven't realized that they bring their values to the workplace, the *shift* is not so difficult. The bigger challenge is when leaders are ambivalent about moving forward with their own psychological development, or are unwilling to move to a new stage. It is more difficult still for those people for whom the challenge is too scary and they struggle to even begin.

The key is the question is, 'Are you sufficiently in touch with who you are and are you willing to explore that?' If you're not willing, don't bother starting. You have to be willing to dig deep because the external changes in the culture of the organization are a reflection of your internal changes.

Stephen Denning, a former Programme Director at World Bank, added:

If you don't have that [Level 4 or 5] mindset, it doesn't matter what methodologies, practices or systems you have in place, everything will go astray. It's a different goal for the organization, a different way of structuring work, a different way of co-ordinating work, different values, a different way of communicating and a different way of using metrics. The physical workspaces are also very different from workspaces that were prevalent just ten years ago. Many managers find it difficult to find sufficient time to think differently about the world to make such a *shift*.

Stephen argues that a *shift* in management is as fundamental as the Copernican shift in astronomy when, instead of seeing the earth as the centre of the universe and the sun being as a small object that revolved around it, it was recognized that the sun is huge and the earth is but a small planet on the periphery. The corresponding *shift* in management is to understand that organizations orbit people and mindsets. Level 3 thinking has it the wrong way around:

When you have the right mindset [at the beginning] and you continue with the right mindset, I don't think there is any question that changes are sustainable. On the contrary, if you bring in a manager with the wrong mindset they can destroy the *shift* in an afternoon. It's like a tree that takes years to grow, but you can chop it down in ten minutes.

According to Avivah Wittenberg-Cox, CEO of 20-First, the *shift* is about balancing EQ and IQ:

I think that every company is now shifting in one way, shape or form. Let's put it a different way, they all feel that like they're shifting. Everybody feels like they're dancing around, adapting and shifting in all kinds of ways. I think that a lot of what you're suggesting about Level 4 *shifting* is that, basically, we're being run by a bunch of IQ [cognitive intelligence] people when we need to bring in EQ [emotional intelligence] people.

To me this says, 'we're just feminizing leadership, we're balancing it out.' There was this strange skew towards a purely rational, numbers-driven, chart-driven approach – run mostly by Wall Street and finance people – and we let everything else get ignored. This rebalancing is just a very twenty-first century push to have the other half of the planet come back in – the other half of whom are masculine-feminine, EQ-IQ. We allowed the pendulum to swing too far in favour of IQ, but we are now finding our equilibrium.

2. Motivation

Motivation is related to mindset. Employees who have *shifted* to Level 4 are motivated to excel in everything they do. Employees who are still at the lower levels are not so motivated, engaged, passionate about their work, or purposeful. The difference between an engaged employee and unengaged employee (anchored below Level 4) is well illustrated by David Macleod, a co-founder of the Engage for Success movement in the UK:

There's also something called common sense, and I don't think we should let people get away with management *spiel* on this. It is common sense to accept that if I'm committed and feel involved with all of the things we've spoken about, I am much more likely to go the extra mile and to put in my best effort. If I feel otherwise, then I'm highly likely to try and get around it or beside it. When you can't see me, don't expect me to do anything to give the customer a great experience or to come up with something positive, because I'm just getting my head down and trying to survive.

I recently spoke to someone who said, 'Monday mornings for me are no longer a pleasurable experience simply because of the way everyone is treated.' You just think, 'What an utter waste. We're just throwing away this resource that we need to utilize so as to compete and win. In a sense, in the UK economic sense, you are throwing pound notes off the roof of your office block because the capability to do great things is being wasted.'

His sobering conclusion was that there is still much work to be done to convince leaders that engagement is as important as, what are confusingly termed, the 'hard issues'. The command and control mindset is still the default position that many managers have been schooled in, and they risk being left behind in a world that has moved on without them.

Motivating employees through 'balancing the head and the heart' is explained by former CEO of the Experior Group, Martin Mackay:

Employees want two things, they want clarity and they want engagement. They basically want a balance of the heart and the head from the leader.

On the head side, it's all about clarity. What they want first of all is to understand what the expectations of the business are and what the future direction of the business is. They want to know, 'At what point have we reached on our journey to achieve that future vision?' They want to understand, 'What role do we play?' They want to understand what relevance they have. They want to understand how their contribution is going to be measured. That's on the head side, if you like.

The heart side is about emotional engagement. Do we have a purpose? Do we have a reason to exist over and above making a profit, which is one of the reasons why the business operates, or is there another reason? From an emotional point of view, does the leader demonstrate sufficient emotional engagement, empathy and communication? Is there vulnerability on the part of the leader or is the leader distant and arrogant? Does the leader and the leadership team demonstrate that they really care and that they really understand their people? Do they understand that the autocratic approach to management doesn't work and do they know that it causes people to leave their jobs?

3. Purpose: discovering and following a higher purpose

A sense of being part of a wider sense of purpose that means more than just meeting deadlines or earning a wage are of central importance to harnessing higher levels of motivation and performance. All the evidence behind research for both the *Management Shift* and *Humane Capital* confirms this, but because the concept is abstract and subjective it does not fit into Level 3 thinking. One of the most important insights into understanding the high-performance culture is to understand the importance of matters that are difficult to measure. Purpose is just one such example. Whatever it may be, whether it is a breakthrough technology or a cleaner environment or a caring service, it has to matter to people.

Following his career as HR Director for Unilever, Geoff McDonald has been helping many companies become more purposeful in a way that drives the growth and profitability of the business, but he does so in a caring and conscious way that takes into account the limits of the planet and the significant social challenges the world faces. He said:

> I kind of thought to myself, 'You know, Unilever's not going to save the world on its own. We need many more companies out there to play the same role. Why don't I share with others what I've learnt at Unilever. Let's see whether they are interested in becoming an organization that holds a different lens through which to view capitalism, a lens that is more caring and more conscious?' It's really important to have organizations become more purposeful, but I also want to ensure that the individuals in those organizations are flourishing and that their wellbeing is looked after.

In 2010, Paul Polman, the incoming CEO of Unilever, set out a number of ambitious goals. He wanted to double the size of Unilever, reduce the size of its environmental footprint and enhance its social impact. This created a powerful sense of purpose at the company. The company's values had always promoted health and hygiene, but the company was now committed to sustainability also. This renewed sense of purpose began to liberate people and infused a feeling of pride. People were now working for a company that wanted to do good in the world, but which was still growing in size while increasing levels of profitability.

When Paul took over the share price was in the region of £11 to £12 and the employee engagement scores were in the mid-fifties. Unilever was the tenth most in-demand employer in the UK. Seven years later, according to LinkedIn, Unilever had become the third most in-demand employer in the world, behind Google and Apple. Its engagement scores were in the mid-eighties and its share price was in the region of £27 to £29. Geoff's advice was to embed purpose as a driver of growth and profitability, rather than being a brand and reputation enhancing activity. His advice was to follow these steps:

1   Create an audacious purpose.

2   Quantify that purpose and align it to the core of the business (i.e. the products and services the business offers).

3   Undertake a significant change programme in aligning the infrastructure, whether that's the organization structure, some of the processes or some of the systems. They may all have to be redesigned through the lens of the new sense of purpose.

4   Develop the leaders in your organization so that more of them become Level 4 leaders. Go from having purpose at an individual level to developing leaders with a purpose who impact at the organizational level.

Jules Goddard emphasizes the importance of purpose, and how it is best pursued by changing the performance metrics of the organisation:

One of my clients at the London Business School is Roche, the pharmaceutical firm. They're beginning to think that their financial accounts should focus less on the profitability of their enterprise and more on the number of lives saved and the number lives extended because of their products. Thus, measured performance is based upon human health and life expectancy and I think this will make a huge difference to the way in which people behave and think. As a by-product, it will also produce an even more profitable, successful and impactful enterprise.

I do think that most organizations, certainly those I work with at LBS, are chasing the wrong numbers. A small shift in the measurement metric can make a huge difference in behaviour and purpose. As a logical consequence, the narrative in terms of how companies communicate with the capital markets needs to be changed. It ought to be framed in terms of the purpose the organization is trying to serve and the problems it's trying to solve. In this way, profit ceases to be solely about money and, instead, it is seen as a reward for serving a noble purpose.

There's a lot of evidence to support *the oblique principle*, the idea that we achieve our goals indirectly – for example, by serving a purpose we become more profitable. The two goals are not in the least incompatible. The City [of London] needs a different kind of story from the ones they are being told by the firms they're investing in, a more interesting story, a more inspiring story and a nobler story than the one they tend to get from companies.

Paul Excell, a former Chief Innovation Officer for British Telecom also stresses the importance of purpose, drawing a simple analogy with eating out:

What makes a great restaurant experience? What makes the difference between a good salad and a bad salad? Well, it's the way it's been prepared, it's the experience of the restaurant. Structure can give you one thing, but it's the quality of the people, the quality of the training, the quality of the leadership as well as the quality of the people that we don't see. Those people in the back office who prepare the food together with those people who interact with us make a difference, and they are the reason why you'll come back again – or not.

You need to start with a purpose, create a framework and engage your people capacity around that – purposeful people who make a difference. Talented people don't want to work for someone who's not trying to *shift*. You will find yourself in a double whammy situation if you can't hire the people you need to take your business and transform it in the right way, and to keep on transforming it. This is essential for growth and success.

4. Values: Focusing on core values and aligning individual and organizational values

A sense of purpose without values can encourage people to do the right thing in the wrong way, perhaps by taking short cuts or by breaking the law. Inherent values guide people on how to behave in ambiguous or unexpected situations while providing people with the assurances that principled behaviour will always be supported and unethical behaviour will always be challenged. As Dov Seidman, founder of the US consultancy LRN, said:[2]

> In a place without regulations, people do bad things because there is no law against it. In a place with values and principles that guide the company, these will guide it through both difficult times and good times.

His analysis indicates that as few as three per cent of organizations are genuinely guided by strong values. David Macleod, of Engage for Success in the UK, says that too many organizations display their values on the wall, but only pay lip service to those values:

> If those values on the wall and the behaviours that I observe overlap, you get trust or, as we used to call it, integrity. If what the boss says doesn't seem to reflect what I observe in behavioural terms, that gap is called distrust and if you ever work in a distrustful organization, as I have, you will find that you never have enough resources, everyone second-guesses each other and everything takes forever.

In the best organizations, people get on with things because they trust in the reason why they're being asked to do it, and they trust they'll be supported if they take innovative steps, even if they don't achieve 100 per cent at the first attempt. A boss in an organization that has strong values will treat you well and coach you, your voice will be heard and respected. It's not necessarily a democracy, but your voice does count. Above all, there is little or no gap between what is said and what is done.

When Karin Tenelius, a CEO of Tuff Leadership Training, helps organizations to *shift* to a Level 4 culture, she emphasizes the importance of values, but ensures that a high level of communication exists across the organization. The thing that must be done is to distinguish values while setting ground rules. The questions that are raised in respect of inter-relationships and methods of operation must also be addressed in terms of the long-term perspective.

5. *Alignment: Aligning people and systems – leveraging technology through intelligent organizational design*

Aligning people to systems and technology that supports their work is another important element that humanizes organizations. For the past twenty years or so, certainly since the internet was established, futurists have projected the prospect of a paradise of an information-rich, automated world of smart cars, smart buildings and smart workplaces.

Progress has tended to come in short bursts, for example during the period from 2008 to 2012 when a critical mass of people purchased smart phones and tablets. These gadgets are now ubiquitous, but in some respects this is only the beginning.

Dramatic social changes have also begun to flow from the rising number of mobile, connected individuals and, especially, knowledge workers. This is having a huge impact on organizations, workplaces and the role of managers.

However, while the contours of the next burst, such as driverless cars, may be discernible, the timing is difficult to predict.

Mobile technology is making a huge impact on the way we work. The static, formal office is disappearing in many sectors and is being replaced by more mobile teams of people. Managers will have to be much better communicators and motivators now that they are unable to rely on the fear spawned by command and control techniques. The workplace will become more diverse with workers more dispersed.

To get the best out of technology we have to get the best out of people. Inventions should be our tools, not our masters. The reason why new technology sometimes frustrates is because we haven't always modernized our management approaches in line with these advances. We often have intelligent technology, but sub-optimal deployment of human intelligence.

If management is poor and the website programmers are not communicating well with product designers and the marketing guys, the atmosphere in the workplace will become tense and the customer experience correspondingly poor. However, by humanizing organizations managers will get the best out of their people and the best out of their technology. The key areas in which technology supports people are identified by Rob Wirszycz:

Current technologies allow communications to be instantaneous and more personal. One of the companies I mentor is an *ideation* business that has just concluded a large program with a large UK airline in which 20,000 employees were asked how they could improve the on-boarding process, i.e. getting people from the kerbside to the airplane as efficiently as possible. The programme highlighted some fantastic ideas that the management were unaware of.

Another area is the use of technology to observe behaviour. One of the great things about big data is that you can now track people's behaviour online. You can track how people interact, find out where they are, what they're feeling and so on. If you use data in a knowing and positive way you can do the right things better and where there are obstacles to your data management this data can help you to highlight where those obstacles are and remove them before they become a real issue.

6. *Self-organization: fostering the self-organization of engaged employees in communities*

By definition, an empowered organization held together by strong values and a sense of purpose does not consist of units that are under the strict control of a senior manager. These units flourish with a degree of autonomy for both the team and the individuals. This is essential if creativity, innovation, teamwork and a common purpose are to be nurtured, but this does not mean that an anarchic *anything goes* regime is introduced. There are boundaries and there is some order, but there are few rules and the team polices itself.

In previous chapters, examples abound about how this can be made to work in practice, the most evolved self-organizing teams do not even establish a set number of days' holiday per employee. In the consensus opinion of the thought leaders I interviewed for this book, the belief is that empowered teams are essential to make Level 4 work and to enhance sustainability. David Macleod, of the UK's Engage for Success organisation, said:

> I believe that if organizations are going to compete they need to harness the full creativity, the full capability and the full potential of their people. If they want to give great customer service, it's not the organization that gives it, it's the individual employees on the front line who do that. If individual employees come up with innovative ideas, they need to be the ones who see those ideas through (although senior people often front case studies on that innovation).

David holds out that only highly-engaged employees will put in the extra effort to think creatively about how they can best create and enhance the products and services their organization offers and how they can best meet the needs of customers and society. According to David, the critical factors for creating successful, engaging organizations include:

1   Create a strategic narrative, i.e. a story that employees can hold in their heads about where they have been in the past, where they are in the present and where they're trying to go in the future. The one story that everyone's heard of is the story about President Kennedy saying to the chap at NASA who's standing next to his broom, 'What's your job?' He replied, 'My job, Mr President, Sir, is to help put a man on the Moon.'

2   Discuss what success would look like. Employees need to feel that they're treated as human beings and not as human resources. Provide feedback and coaching.

3   Give employees a voice. Successful organizations help employees articulate their views, they do not ignore them. If you are a low-trust organization and you want to improve it, then one of the very first things to do is to make people feel that their ideas are being heard.

4   Pin the organizational values to a wall.

5   Find the parts of an organization that are engaged and see what is going on (engage the intuitive right side of the brain).

6   Review all of the evidence on the benefits of engagement (engage the data processing left side of the brain).

The power of engagement is also illustrated by Richard Barrett of Barrett's Value Centre. He said:

As employee engagement went up, every other indicator improved. As cultural entropy went down, every other indicator improved. Thus, revenues increased (that is, income per employee), productivity improved and the share price went up. Then, in 2008 when there this economic bump came along, the companies that were doing this were able to respond more quickly than others.

7. *A caring ethos*

The values referred to in the earlier section ought to include the value of nurturing and caring for everyone in the organization. People should never be seen as a means to an end, they should be seen as equal citizens deserving of dignity and respect. A truly empowered organization that operates at Level 4 or 5 will nurture a sense of purpose for each individual, as well as for the organization as a whole. There will be an expectation of performance, but this will be based on the needs of the customer rather than the meeting of arbitrary targets. In return, the organization should be a safe and creative place with high levels of trust. The few rules that do exist should include those that are designed to protect vulnerable people. Jules Goddard of the London Business School adds:

> There are three objectives that underpin why UK companies need to make the *shift*, or if they have already made the *shift*, why they need to reinforce that *shift* and work even harder to reach Level 5. These objectives are commercial, social and moral.
>
> The commercial reason? There is increasing evidence that a link exists between humane practices and economic performance. I think it comes through the provision of an environment that meets three profound needs in human beings: a sense of identity, a sense of purpose and a sense of belonging. It's only a Level 4 or a Level 5 organization that addresses these needs. We go to work not to make a living but to make a life and unless the organization helps us to build that life, and not just a livelihood, the organization is failing. In a sense, work has replaced the church, the family, the neighbourhood and the community as a place where we find purpose, identity and a sense of belonging.

The social reason why the *shift* must be made is that the next generation will be impatient with organizations that cannot meet their needs, and those organizations that are unable to recruit and retain the best talent are going to lose out.

Finally, it's the right and moral thing to do. The golden rule that you treat others as you want to be treated yourself is at the heart of what is described as the *shift*. We need to treat people as the 'ends' and not the 'means', while being aware of the realism that demands that we recognize the traditional management view that people should be managed as factors of production, just like capital or raw materials. Indeed, we use the phrase *human resources*.

I think there's a huge distinction between treating people as a human resource and treating people as resourceful humans, and it's a rare organization that acknowledges this distinction and acts upon it. Another conceptual error is to describe employees as *working for the company*. It should be the other way around, the company works for individual human beings who have come together to do things that they couldn't do individually. The organization is the means and its members are the ends. Whenever we lapse into thinking of employees as the raw material of the organization, we make a profound moral and philosophical mistake.

David Macleod describes how one motivator for him was seeing talented people working in toxic environments. People who felt disengaged, disempowered and who had a relatively poor level of wellbeing. He said:

When you investigate the situation, you often find that the cause has nothing to do with the company being in difficult straits, it is down to how employees are treated in their workplace. It is the mindset and conduct of the managers that determines whether the workplace has a toxic or a healthy environment.

Among the worst effects of those who work in an unhealthy environment is the impact this has on their home lives. They become less at one with themselves, less fulfilled, less happy, less engaged and their personal relationships can be damaged by this condition. We really can't afford to have a situation where the contribution of people is diminished and, from a human perspective, what an awful waste it is to have people unhappy because of the way they're treated at work.

8. *Organizational learning processes*

One of the reasons for linking the *Management Shift* concept of five levels of performance to organizational indicators in the 6 Box Leadership Model is to ensure that a move to a higher level is both organization-wide and sustainable, otherwise there would be a risk that higher levels of engagement would be too reliant on a single leader. To sustain performance and behaviours at the higher levels, the most enlightened organizations first establish their purpose and their values, but they must then ensure that their processes are strong and that learning is on-going, to the extent that these values will outlive any particular group of managers. Thus, the eighth key theme the data analysis reveals is a commitment to continual organizational learning.

Communication is the key building block of a learning organization. This is well explained by Arie de Geus. He likens a human community to a human organism that is highly complex and held together by healthy communication, in the same way that cells and neurons maintain body and brain functioning. In both cases, much of the internal communication is hard-wired. In a supra-human community consisting of human individuals, the principal method of interaction is language. One of the things Wittgenstein [a former Professor of Philosophy at the University of Cambridge] said is, 'If you don't ever work for it, you can't understand it, you can't hear it and you can't see it.'

Arie argues that many senior managers have a similar background to their contemporaries, which can be a serious incumbrance:

For instance, if they are all chemical engineers they speak the language of chemical engineering, or if they are accountants they speak the language of money, but the language they speak does not reflect the reality they deal with. If you begin to see that and understand that, you are also beginning to understand why so many of these situations go totally wrong. If some of the realities that come out of the world do not fall within their vocabulary, then they won't have a word for it and they cannot see it. Language creates reality. That means that if you are looking for diversity in the composition of the learning circles in your human community, you also need women. They add another vocabulary to the group which makes it more diverse, and being more diverse means they now have a richer language than they had before. They see more.

Curtis Carlson, a former CEO of the Stanford Research Institute (SRI) is now working with large organizations and governments to help them to develop learning organizations that foster innovation. He found that one key issue is, perhaps, under-recognized and it's one that the collective ability has to prioritize:

Basically it's a simple set of principles, but they are fundamental. If you don't do them you have a real problem. First is to focus on important problems, not just the ones that interest you. Most people waste their time on interesting problems because they haven't yet defined what important means to their enterprise. From working with many companies around the world, we've found generally less than twenty per cent of what they were working on had hardly any value at all. In other words, most of what companies do is a complete waste.

The second principle, he argues, is to encourage innovation and the creation of value, he made reference to a *value creation playbook*:

Many organizations attempt to teach teamwork, collaboration, communication skills, project management, Six Sigma and so on, but they do not have a process for teaching innovation. A *value creation playbook* consists of definitions, concepts, tools, processes and productive team practices. For example, it spells out the definition for a value proposition based on how a customer would view the issue. Basic and essential questions are asked, such as 'What is important to the customer and market? Does our offering and business model meet that? What are the benefits (relative to costs) from offering a superior product to those offered by the competition and other alternatives?'

Innovation is about learning. As soon as you say *learn fast*, you realize that everything you can do to accelerate learning is good. When you introduce things that slow it down – barriers and inappropriate authoritarian management – all of the benefits are eliminated. You must understand that the people doing the work must learn fast and that if you stop them from doing so you're putting your enterprise at great risk.

To support his work, he set up value creation forums. People come together every two to eight weeks; they stand up before their peers and present the value propositions of the projects they are working on. They are then critiqued by their colleagues. These should be positive meetings based on identifying what is good and providing the means for improvement.

These forums provide ways to discuss, address and ultimately remove unwanted pathways that can exist within an organization, e.g. the bureaucratic stricture that requires employees to seek permission from the company hierarchy before communicating ideas to another division.

Innovation is the primary driver of growth, prosperity, new jobs, social progress and the funding for social programmes. Without innovation, all those things will decline. Jules Goddard argues that to instil organizational learning one has to transform the vocabulary of these organizations:

The controlling mentality is one that talks about targets, KPIs and incentives. A learning organization talks more about questions, hypotheses and experiments. I think both are necessary, but the bias in British business tends to be towards control and away from learning. A Level 4 organization would keep some of those controls in place, but would emphasize the asking of better questions, the generation of more interesting ideas and the conduct of more courageous experiments.

How these findings can be implemented in *your* organization

There isn't a single tool or programme that can transform an organization from a sub-optimal Level 3 workplace to a high-performance one. Without support from a senior level it is unlikely that much progress can be made, other than in a team that is already semi-autonomous and typically comprised of people with similar skills and qualifications.

Where there is commitment at the top level of an organization, change can be profound, even transformational, but in order to sustain this higher level of awareness and performance it is helpful to use the 6 Box Leadership Model online diagnostics (which involves all levels of the organization). The evidence presented in this chapter supports an approach that sustains organizational learning and the formation of a collaborative strategy based on strong values. These benefits are fixed and will outlive any cadre of leaders.

The rest of this chapter outlines the practical steps required for implementation, based on *Humane Capital* research. They are grouped into four broad categories, and are illustrated in Figures 6.2, 6.3, 6.4 and 6.5.

1   Individual shift,

2   Discovering and following a higher purpose,

3   Developing engagement,

4   Fostering innovation.

Individual Shift: Changing the mindset of leaders and employees

As Chris Shern found, the first principle is:

> Get out of a toxic environment. If your situation presents you with major barriers, but you wish to operate in an empowered Level 4 way and your working experience is toxic, you may wish to consider a radical alternative to your work and life balance. You need to be in a place that has at least some opportunity for personal development.

You may already have started your mindset *shift* towards seeing healthy organizations and employees as being empowered and learning continuously,

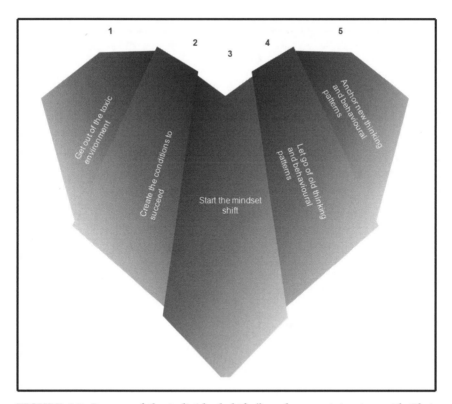

FIGURE 6.2 *Process of the individual shift (based on an interview with Chris Shern).*

perhaps through a course, a talk or reading a book such as this one. This means that you are already developing the personal confidence to hold creative and innovative ideas and to take the lead in areas where you have knowledge and expertise. It also means that you are ditching the old ways of thinking that required one having to request permission to explore every idea or initiative. Once the virtuous circle is established, the new way of thinking and operating becomes anchored.

Discovering and following a higher purpose

All of the research confirms that a strong sense of purpose, one that extends and expands into society far beyond the short-term linear indicators of sales

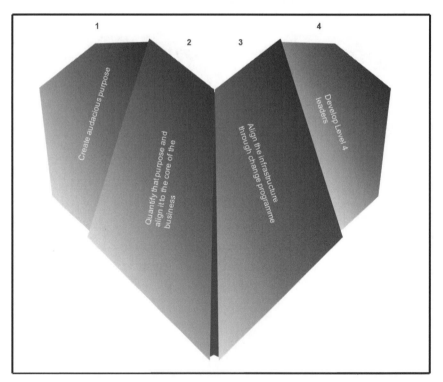

FIGURE 6.3 *Process of identifying and leveraging purpose (based on an interview with Geoff McDonald).*

and profits, is key to encouraging the highest levels of performance. An audacious but realistic aim lies at the centre of this approach. This sense of purpose can be tested as the organization builds and aligns its infrastructure and change programme around it. The final outcome is the development of empowering Level 4 leaders.

Developing engagement

Once the aims are established and the leadership development is in progress, the real work of building an engaging culture begins, and this will have many

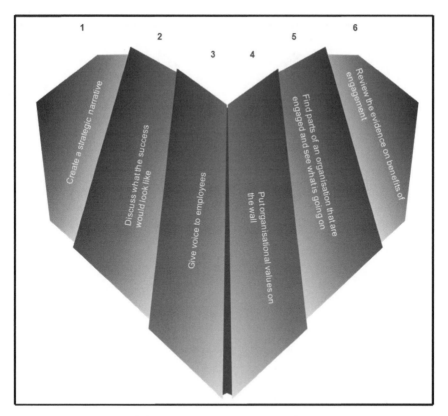

FIGURE 6.4 *Process of developing engaging culture (based on an interview with David Macleod).*

dimensions. It means establishing core values and making sure that they are exhibited at an individual and organizational level. There should then be a move towards an organization that is comprised of a network of empowered teams rather than a rigid set of hierarchies. The principles should encompass a caring ethos and should foster continuous organizational learning as an on-going discipline.

Fostering innovation

As discussed earlier in this chapter, Level 4 and Level 5 organizations must develop a collaborative strategy. There should be continual discussion about

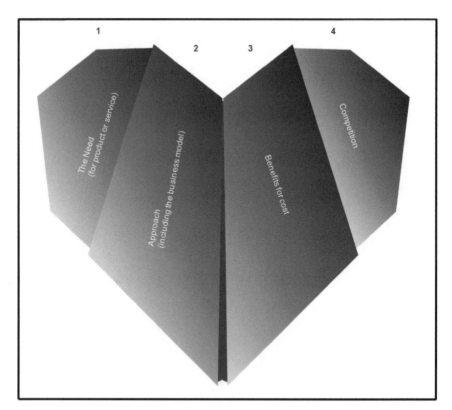

FIGURE 6.5 *Process for fostering innovation (based on an interview with Curtis Carlson).*

future choices throughout the entire network of teams that constitute the organization, with all of these choices based upon the customer's perspective. Honest mistakes should go unpunished and should be treated as opportunities to fix things and to learn. Innovation should be encouraged at all levels in a multiplicity of disciplines that not only embrace technology, but also include forms of service delivery, product design and methods of communicating. Value creation forums can greatly assist in this. (See the interview with Curtis Carlson in Chapter 6.)

 SEVEN REFLECTION POINTS FROM THIS CHAPTER

1 An empowered working or leadership style cannot flourish in a toxic environment. Do your leadership development programmes address the context as well as the individual's capabilities?

2 What measures have you put in place to ensure that your staff have a wider sense of purpose, one that goes beyond monetary reward?

3 Does your organization prioritize ethical means as well as ethical ends? Is your way of working a priority in itself?

4 Does your organization genuinely care about the people working with it, or does it view of people as resources?

5 Do you create autonomous teams that innovate and respond to customers?

6 Does your organization maintain a continuous discipline of high levels of engagement, performance and continuous learning?

7 A blame culture can kill engagement and innovative capacity. Does your organization have a forgiving attitude towards honest mistakes, treating them as opportunities to learn?

7

Creating positive ripples: the few affect the whole

'Each time a person stands up for an ideal, or acts to improve the lot of others, they send forth a tiny ripple of hope ... These ripples build a current which can sweep down the mightiest walls of oppression and resistance.' Robert F. Kennedy

---

KEY INSIGHTS FROM THIS CHAPTER

- Creating humane workplaces is a moral duty.
- Humane workplaces are diverse, inclusive and collaborative. They attract the best talent.
- The value of the *shift* to the creation of humane workplaces is immense.
- There are still many barriers to humanizing organizations.
- Maintaining the status quo has dire consequences.
- The time for action is now.

Shifting the mindset and the organizational culture to create more humane workplaces

The concept of *human resources* is an inert and inaccurate metaphor. In the real workplace people are both emotional and intelligent, moreover we continually communicate with and thereby influence each other. We always have an influence, whether positive or negative, but it is almost never neutral. Once you understand this, you've begun to make the *shift* in mindset towards unleashing *humane capital*. It is an empowering insight. You can say to yourself, 'What I do, say, decide and communicate today and every other day affects my team, our customers and the organization.'

Shifting up the levels from Level 2/3 to Level 4/5 creates positive ripples that spread from individuals to their teams, their families, the entire organization and society. We are like energy transmission masts that emit energy with our thoughts, emotions and words. Evidence for this is not just empirical. Research in neuroscience shows that our thoughts and emotions affect the heart's magnetic field, which in turn affects our environment whether we are conscious of this or not. We pick up the moods and attitudes of those around us through our *mirror neurons*, brain cells that operate as a kind of neural Wi-Fi. When we detect someone else's emotions through their actions, our *mirror neurons* reproduce those emotions whether we intend them to or not. Such transmissions occur at both the conscious and subconscious levels. When we are anchored at the lower levels (Levels 1, 2 and 3) we create negative ripples. When we are anchored at higher levels (Levels 4 and 5) we create positive ripples. A relatively small number of people can affect the whole.

Lord David Evans, Chairman of the Institute of Collaborative Working and founder of one of the largest printing businesses in Europe observed:

> Because of all the advantages, I think it's absolutely vital that we move to Level 4, which I've been doing and trying to do for many years. You get better working relationships and you have much more open relationships with both your customers and suppliers. You are much more professional because you understand thoroughly what your clients expect, and you make sure that your suppliers understand what you require of them. It's all about collaboration.

He has some practical tips on communication and collaboration; short meetings and regular communication, because 'everyone gets bored with long meetings.'

It is our moral and ethical duty to create humane workplaces

Jules Goddard of the London Business School argues that the prize for moving to Level 4 and Level 5 at the organizational level is not only about personal fulfilment, it is also about the quality of civilization:

> If we put that at risk by staying with a nineteenth century model of management we're doomed, because other parts of the world will find ways of energizing the human talent at their disposal far more effectively than we can.

He points out that a business is not just a technical system, it's also a social and a moral system. Now that everyone has access to all the information and the knowledge they need, the differentiating factors are the human factor, the quality of interpersonal relationships, the energy that we bring to work and the inspirational way in which we design the workplace. It's the context in which we work that creates the productivity. Management and leadership are less about directing human beings and more about the design of a setting in which virtuous and creative behaviour becomes the norm, not the exception:

> There's no mystique about management. It isn't a secret form of knowledge. It's about being human, it's about connectedness and it's about empathy. If there is an intellectual skill there is also an emotional skill. It is the skill of *mentalization*, the ability to read others' minds and to see the world through the eyes of others. These are critical skills in any Level 4 organization.

A business is a moral community as much as it is an economic or commercial community. If the moral purpose or reason for working is not being addressed, then only the economic purpose remains and, that being so, the organization will then fail.

Attracting talent by ditching the command and control mindset

Before the financial crisis that erupted in 2008–09, investment banking (with all of its lucrative rewards) was one of the most sought-after employment sectors for graduates. Since then other professions have overtaken banking in terms of attractiveness. This marks a clear warning for any business leader who thinks that monetary reward alone is sufficient to attract and retain the most talented and motivated people. As discussed in the previous chapter, people want to have a wider sense of purpose. They do not necessarily want to change the world in a grand way, but they want to make a difference to the quality of life of the people they serve. No one is motivated to do work that makes no difference. Moreover, the way of working, i.e. being empowered to make the most of your talent and to have a say, is a huge motivator.

Sir Paul Judge, the late key benefactor of the Judge Business School at Cambridge University, emphasized the importance of moving away from the command and control approach in order to attract talent:

We are moving towards a world of teamwork. The hierarchies are breaking down. There used to be the old man at the top – and it was usually a man – who told you what to do, but now it is much more complex with a matrix of organizations and people in other continents being tasked with the same project. Managing the complexity has now become a key issue.

He says that most big organizations, such as banks, accounting firms or companies like Unilever, cannot tell people what to do all the time – their organizations are too large and they have to stay responsive. However, since we moved away from command and control management, the cultural trend has changed. People are free to leave and if they are reasonably well-educated there are lots of opportunities. He points out that even in the military there is now much more emphasis on teamwork. He says, metaphorically, 'If you are in an organization that needs innovation, you need the approach of *the research scientist not the airline pilot*':

> You need to explore new opportunities, not follow the established route. You need to encourage creativity because if you do not encourage it you will find yourself in difficulty [when] competing with creative organizations. You have to recognize that employees are the best asset of any company, so must do what is right for your current employees and the employees you wish to attract. That is the key to it.
>
> In different places at different times, you will want to attract different kinds of employees. If you're running a coal mine, that is different to running a consulting company. However, many organizations, such as airlines or the NHS, should have multiple cultures in different areas.

Humanised workplaces are diverse and inclusive

One of the few positive by-products of the banking scandals and financial crises of recent years has been an increased awareness of the importance of psychology in major economic events. It is increasingly apparent that collective cognitive biases contributed to excessive risk-taking in the banking industry.

Confirmation bias, which is the tendency to filter out or disregard unwelcome evidence while clinging to preferred narratives, and Groupthink, the tendency to think alike and echo one another's prejudices, are two biases that are closely linked to a lack of diversity. As Arie de Geus noted in the previous chapter, if all or most of the board and senior management are male and from similar disciplines, commonly accountancy or engineering, there exists a lack of diversity in the way problems are addressed. This is a serious weakness.

Level 4 and 5 workplaces are humane, diverse and inclusive. Dame Fiona Woolf, a former Lord Major of the City of London and a distinguished champion for inclusion and diversity, observed:

> I think the original paradigm demonstrated that diversity was really a matter of fairness and equality. My thinking has since moved. It is a business imperative to include all the talent in the team that you can, and to focus on how best to capture that diversity. Diversity means difference, but how do you capture the benefits of diversity? After all, if we all come from the same background and the same schools and the same universities, where are the new ideas going to come from?
>
> A leader should not be thought of as someone at the top of a tree in a command and control environment. Genuine leadership is much more participative. It is about collaboration, bringing people in, and including people and encouraging them to make the most of their abilities. Leaders at all levels of an organization need to find ways to accept and deal with these differences. While many organizations now feature diversity inclusion initiatives – including training on subconscious biases and mentoring schemes – they will have limited impact unless they are embedded into the organizational culture.

While there is a business case for diversity, it should not be thought of as a means to an end, Dame Woolf said:

> I think that the fairness and equality issues should not be overlooked. We worry a lot about social mobility and I think that if we don't use this

management shift, which you've demonstrated so well in your earlier book, we will find that we can't move on with our social mobility agenda. We're missing out on doing something that I think is very important for society, which is to help everybody, whatever their background, reach their full potential. If we don't, we're storing up social problems and social unrest for the future. Society does not function at its best if does not capture all the talent that it has within it. There are people who are held back simply because of lack of opportunity at the starting point. As regards social unrest there is commonly a trigger, usually because disadvantaged people are unable to access to the workplace. Yet there's talent in these disadvantaged people, which both society and the workplace could benefit from.

When I was president of the Law Society, when we looked at the key motivational factors that keep people in their jobs, none of these included pay and conditions or work-life balance or flexible working. Of the top two motivators, number one was the quality of supervision and the ability to develop skills, and number two was access to top-quality work.

Collaboration becomes a way of life, including for strategy development

It follows from the principles discussed in this book – high performance levels, strong values and purpose, and learning instilled at an institutional level – that development of strategy should be collaborative. Level 3 thinking sees strategy as being a twice-yearly discussion confined to board level. This is a hopelessly inadequate approach that is unable to deal with fast-changing markets, as well as being elitist and hierarchical. A genuinely innovative organization has open, healthy forums at all levels throughout the organization that constantly shape and reshape strategy. David Macleod of Engage for Success critiques the *ivory tower* approach:

I remember a Korean professor of business saying, 'Western cognac-drinking bosses spend far too much time in the boardroom. The answers are all to be found at the front line.' When I took over this business and realized what state it was in, I thought I'd follow his advice and I spent a lot of time at the front line.

The traditional issues that senior executives on the board still concern themselves with remain: which markets to be in, which to withdraw from, profit margins, the cost base and cash management. However, all of these need interests need to be supplemented by an equal concern as to whether employees understand, own and are committed to that strategy, otherwise the organization has a fundamental weakness. Lord David Evans is an advocate for collaboration, humanized workplaces and the development of business partnerships:

We had an open situation with our employees where we encouraged feedback. We had incentives for our employees. We treated the whole business like a family and worked very closely with our employees to develop them, to train them and to have open communications.

We also had open relationships with our suppliers and we had an open tendering process whereby people knew exactly what they were up against when it came to providing a service. That didn't mean disclosing the pricing, it meant giving feedback. We worked in partnership with our customers, kept them informed and remained open late at night because in those old days – the dark old days when printing staff often went home at five o'clock – we wanted to provide a comprehensive service.

This was one of the reasons why we grew very quickly into being a major player in the British printing industry. It's a field I passionately believe in and that's the whole tenet. The principles of the businesses I've been involved with have all encouraged a different way of working, an open way of working, where you work in partnership with your customers, suppliers and your staff, which in turn helps to develop your staff. What does that bring? It brings great loyalty. I hesitate to use the word *family*, but it brings a close relationship with one's employees that you can build upon so that you get back what you put in, which I very much believe in.

One helpful discipline in instilling such a healthy approach is to have a no blame culture, one where people are not punished for making an honest mistake. People should feel free to own up to a mistake, which then allows everyone to work together to overcome the problem. There should be no recriminations like there used to be. This is a new way of working. It works. It saves a lot of money.

The value of the *Big Shift* towards *humane capital*

Ample evidence is emerging from this and other research studies that both individuals and organizations can obtain huge advantages when they go through the *shift* and start to work in humane organizations. One of the greatest returns comes from the commercial and financial benefits that are created, as well as talent retention. Lord Evans' business partner, Caroline Minshell, emphasizes the importance of focusing on people:

> We are only are as good as the people who work for us and represent us to our clients. I think the testament to that was that the staff turnover at Centurion – as I say, we had about 150 employees – was about one per cent. They stayed forever. When we did the 360 appraisals they appraised us and we appraised them, which was all quite fun, but I think it also helped everybody the recognize the value of being part of the organization.

Table 7.1 shows quotes from interviewees about the value of the *Management Shift*, while Figure 7.1 shows excerpts from the key messages about the value of the *Big Shift* for individuals and organizations.

TABLE 7.1 *The value of the* shift *towards humane organizations*

Examples of quotes on the value (price tag) of the *shift*	Interviewee
It is **priceless**	Geoff McDonald, Paul Excell, Graeme Nuttall, Kevin O'Brian, Jack Hubbard, Kalyan Madabhushi, Simon La Fosse, Tom Rippin
About **ten per cent of the market value** *of any business*	Jules Goddard
If they are not attractive, they will not be able to recruit the people they want. If you are command and control company in, for instance, consulting, **nobody is going to work for you**	Sir Paul Judge
Look at future state and where you are now and make a **saving calculation** *after the shift*	Rob Wirszycz
Given that disengaged employees are a massive cost, then it is one of the **very best investments** *an organization can make*	David Macleod
One can get close to saying it is worth an **extra ten per cent, fifteen per cent of turnover**	Graeme Nuttall
It is **limitless**	Fiona Woolf
There is no price for **magic**	Simon Fowler
It would lead to a richer vocabulary. The richer vocabulary would lead to seeing more and more being made aware of what happens in the world outside. The rules of the decision-making language game leads to faster decisions and, almost certainly, better quality decisions. In Shell you talk about **millions** *immediately!*	Arie de Geus
What is it going to cost you to hire someone [a CEO] who has that belief and personal commitment? You may need to change your whole leadership team to get to a place where you can make this happen. That can cost a lot of money, but **the rewards are so high**	Stephen Ball

Examples of quotes on the value (price tag) of the *shift*	Interviewee
*What happens is **efficiency goes up and profitability goes up**. There is a high quality service and happier customers. Innovation happens. So there are so many good things that come out of this. On-going learning – people develop, people grow. Constant improvements are made because people in organizations can't stand not inventing improvements. It also gives them a stable place where you're not so vulnerable to shifts in economy or competition from others. There are so many benefits It's hard to set a price because there's so many aspects of it in the long-run*	Karin Tenelius
*On the spiritual level I couldn't agree with you more and if you visit the people at SRI they will tell you that their **lives have been transformed** and that it's a completely different place now – very few of our people have left. So that's another economic argument. The reason they didn't leave is they wouldn't have that same kind of freedom, experience and achievement in other companies. They wouldn't be treated the way we treat people. They wouldn't have the opportunity to make a big impact*	Curtis Carlson
*Is there any price for **happiness**? There is no price tag for happiness*	Chris Shern
*Depending on the size of the company, it is worth **millions and millions of pounds or dollars**. The rate of return on cultural transformation must be thousands and thousands per cent. The costs are quite small when you are talking about the impact that such things have on the organization as a whole – and its profitability*	Richard Barrett
*The main value is **life as opposed to death**. Organizations won't survive in their current state, so this is a way to be prosperous in a world in which the balance of power has shifted from the seller to the buyer, and if they don't make this shift then they are not long for this world*	Steve Denning
*Without putting an exact price tag on it, I would say it's a difference between mere existence and **true happiness***	Doug Kirkpatrick
*More than **$1 million***	Jack Bergstrand

(continued)

TABLE 7.1 *(Continued)*

Examples of quotes on the value (price tag) of the *shift*	Interviewee
*The benefits of moving society in that direction is a question of society **being able to function or not** for everybody in the long term. So the big price for all of us is to eradicate poverty and put issues like climate change behind us. There is no alternative. In the short term, we might get away with it, but some companies will be flushed out earlier than others. Longer term, if we don't make a balance with nature in terms of addressing climate change and if we don't live in balance with fellow human beings and address issues of inequality, we will drive ourselves to a situation that I don't think you want to discuss*	Paul Polman
You can't buy it	Ajaz Ahmed, Sam Kelly
*Look at the valuation. Look at the increase in value of Handelsbanken shares since 1970 compared to the index for European banks. Look at the **value creation***	Anders Bouvin
*It's really in **tens of millions***	Celine Schilinger
*Customers will come to you if they know you do the right thing and you're a good company. If you exhibit Level Four characteristics, **you'll grow**. That is the by-product of performing Level 4 properly*	Charlie Isaacs
*So whatever you earn, the biggest reward as a whole is spending quality time with the people you want to be with. In a way it is leading them to the **peaceful place** they want to be. So the price tag is not important*	Dana Denis-Smith
*The real answer is what's **the price tag on your company?** Like if your company disappears, what's is it worth to prevent that?*	John Stepper
*From an organizational perspective, **costs** [in a Level 4 organisation] are **twenty per cent lower** than the average organization. So you have a very healthy margin and you have a yearly profit that gives you the opportunity to be independent, while having more flexibility*	Jos de Block
*If you're simply looking at getting employees to feel part of the system and being truly engaged, that will reduce attrition. It will also make your business more **sustainable** and it will reduce your training costs. It's hard to put a number on it, but I think employee engagement is one of the biggest issues for companies today – and it's a big part of sustainability*	Mick Yates

Examples of quotes on the value (price tag) of the *shift*	Interviewee
It would have been like comparing a business that wouldn't even be here anymore to a company that is **extremely successful**, one *which has made £2million over a four-year period. If you project that forward over the next five years and you compare what the company is worth now and what it will be worth in the future, the value could increase ten-fold. So you're talking of up to £20million in value being created. Beyond that, what really matters is that when we look back we can see how happy we were and how we lived our lives, that is priceless*	Jack Hubbard
The value is more intangible that tangible. I see it from different angles. (1) I am able to **attract extremely good talent** *– the best people give you the best results. (2) There is an aligned collective purpose. (3) There is creativity and innovation and I feel that, overall, that's* **priceless**	Kalyan Madabhushi
That is how we moved from being a $700million company to **$4billion** *today, with a market capitalization of $1.4billion*	Vineet Nayar
I don't start from a price tag approach, but I would say it's got to be seen as you're almost buying a **license to go on operating in the twenty-first century**. *Otherwise, why would people want to come and work with you?*	Martin Donnelly
For me the benefit is that more learners flourish more often, that **more dreams are fulfilled** *more often, that more staff feel more fulfilled more often and that we have more leaders than before – and they are better leaders than we had in the past*	Paul Little
It's absolutely **inestimable**. *It is whether employees have an emotional engagement with the brand*	Martin Mackay
The value depends on the market. If you have a changeable market in which responsiveness is highly valued, then a shift becomes very valuable. In fact, as **valuable as the entire destruction of the company**	Helen Walton, Paul Dolman-Darrall
There is no need of a price tag for human-centric, value creation processes. They are priceless	Stelio Verzera
It would be **invaluable** *for us. We wouldn't exist without it*	Michael Goethe

(*continued*)

TABLE 7.1 *(Continued)*

Examples of quotes on the value (price tag) of the *shift*	Interviewee
*It would be a **really high price** for me personally because I really like my life now. On the business side of it, we have built a very valuable company based on these principles, with continuity in contracts, continuity in relationships and high profitability*	Gerwin Schuring
*It's **profoundly important***	Peter Cheese
*Well managed companies on average outperform those that aren't by, let's say, at least twenty-three per cent. So, if you accept that the average life of a company is about fifteen years and suppose your company did £1M sales annually, if they became a better managed company they could do about £1.2M of sales a year for 15 years. The value to that company, undiscounted, would obviously be greater. The additional productivity of the **extra £200K a year** over fifteen years would be accumulated*	Ann Francke
*It's invaluable. It has a **price tag of infinity** because, to me, the shift is fundamental to organizations that are going to be sustainable*	Rick Wartzman
*Better management creates **better long-term value***	Richard Straub
*Example: **A forty per cent reduction in turnover of staff** over a period of two to three years*	Rob Noble
***Twenty to twenty-five per cent of our revenues** are coming as a result of this shift*	Michael Jenkins
Twenty to thirty per cent of turnover** in those organizations minimum. In some less profitable ones, probably **the difference between survival and prosperity	Nigel Girling

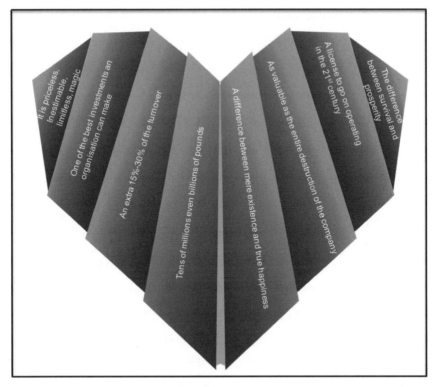

FIGURE 7.1 *Selection of quotes on the value of the* Big Shift *to Level 4.*

When done comprehensively and with integrity, the *shift* that we describe in this book is experienced at the individual and at the collective level, with different constituencies gaining simultaneously. This way of thinking is in contrast with earlier managerial models that assumed that one stakeholder would always win at the expense of another – a reductionist and cynical approach that is not borne out by how the highest-performing organizations work. The benefits of the *shift* are financial and commercial, as well as personal and human. As can be seen from the quotes in Table 7.1, many business leaders have been able to assess the financial return from the *shift*, which runs into millions of pounds. In some cases, it has made the difference between survival and bankruptcy. More importantly, it has transformed the quality of life for those people who now work for an organization that has a purpose they believe in and whose leaders encourage and coach them to make the most out of their abilities. For many, this gift is priceless.

If the *Big Shift* is so important, why is it not happening on a large scale?

There is undisputed evidence from this study and many others that the *shift* to a more humanized way of conducting business is not just a matter of business survival, it also helps enterprises to thrive. A growing number of organizations now recognize the importance of a Level 4 culture (Appendix 5 shows a list of those organizations identified as Level 4 organizations by those leaders who were interviewed for this project). Yet, despite the strength of the evidence and the scale of the rewards, for a variety of reasons the *Big Shift* is not happening on a large scale as yet. As part of my analysis for this book, I identified some of the barriers to implementing the move towards *Humane Capital* and the *Management Shift*. The overall conclusion was that the *shift* can be difficult to adopt when the starting point is from a low operating level, where levels of trust are equally low. The previous chapter also emphasized the multidimensional nature of the *shift* – this isn't a quick and easy fix and you can run into problems.

Some of the barriers are summarized as below:

1 *Insufficient or partial effort.*

2 *Lack of a sense of purpose.*

3 *It can sound intangible.*

4 *Communication is poor.*

5 *The business organization is unreformed.*

6 *The leaders are not ready.*

7   *The employees are not ready.*

8   *The effort is perceived as too great.*

9   *It can still sound un-businesslike.*

10   *There remains the perception that work and life are separate.*

The following section describes how these factors have become barriers to the *shift* to *Humane Capital*. These anonymous quotes have been taken from the research.

Insufficient or partial effort.   A partial, or half-hearted approach can result in defeat and retreat on the path towards Level 4. A lack of trust and poor communication creates resistance. If the organization is clearly not open, especially at the leadership and the board level, there's going to be a lot of resistance.

Lack of a sense of purpose.   People need to know what they are working towards and should feel comfortable with those aims. You cannot generate enthusiasm without this. You need to demonstrate a strong sense that they [the organization's leaders] want to obtain all the good things that come along with the *shift*. Another respondent observed, 'You can no longer rely on past business success, you need to be prepared to review ways of working. If the purpose is not clear, or if parts of the organization have become distracted by other objectives that have been incentivized by measures that are not aligned to purpose, people lose sight of the original objective and are distracted by these other factors.' Sometimes, performance management is not linked to purpose and in many organizations the strategic direction is in any case unclear. 'If people are not confident about their over-riding purpose it is difficult to bring others along. People need to work at building a good culture.' An organization that has experienced a significant merger or successive acquisitions can struggle to identify or create a unifying sense of purpose.

It can sound intangible. While a positive organizational culture feels positive once you are in it, the benefits are manifold with many of them being financial (see the quotes in Table 7.1). The move towards the *shift* can sound vague, which is why I set out a practical road map in the previous chapter. Observations from my interviews included comments such as, 'it's difficult to measure trust' and 'intangible concepts such as culture are difficult for people to grasp.' Other views stated that, 'people need to find new ways to connect and to engage, and trust is a powerful emotion that can only be built slowly and surely.' While there are many practical steps that can be taken, altering mindset is, in part, a subconscious and cultural challenge. However, trust and engagement can be measured. As one respondent pointed out, 'Many organizations don't know that trust is measurable and definable and that it is a very strong indicator.' However, another interviewee commented that more effort is required to create measures for non-financial objectives.

Communication is poor. The move to a higher level doesn't just happen, and planning is not enough. There has to be sustained communication throughout the teams, not just edicts from the top. Some of the observations beneath this heading were:

1 [There are] outdated views of communication. It is no longer appropriate to have perfect press releases, which now have a level of transparency that everyone can check.

2 It's a challenge to develop clear, transparent and authentic communication.

The business organization is unreformed. While mindset and attitude lie at the heart of the *shift*, it can be difficult to make progress if the business structure itself is unreformed or if formal permission from the top of the silo is still required to permit collaboration with other departments. This can result in *pulling the wrong levers.* For example, 'You need to restructure, sometimes radically, to realign.' A devolved business set-up can be perceived as being too risky, with senior managers being concerned, reasonably or otherwise, that others *might run off and do silly things,* or they may worry whether customer-facing staff can take responsibility for making major decisions. This point underlines the need for training and preparation. Most organizations have been designed by men who are schooled in task-orientation and IQ. A lack of gender balance can further exacerbate this.

There are also risks associated with moving to a decentralized structure, especially when quality standards and health and safety issues are important concerns. '[We] cannot respond to the need to *shift* from a command and control environment without retaining control of essential health and safety disciplines.' Safety is generally enhanced with a move to high trust and Level 4, but the transition may require sensitive handling and appropriate training.

'It's very difficult for a plc to change to a culture like Virgin. Even [Richard] Branson had to make it private again.' There remains the dehumanizing concept of people being viewed as resources in much business planning and thinking. Many workplace cultures are still rooted in the enslaving concept of people working *for* the company.

The leaders are not ready. Some business leaders 'have difficulty moving ahead with their own psychological development, or are unwilling to do so'. Some perceive the required change as too great.

The ego of senior executives can be a factor. If they are in a senior position and are well paid, they may perceive that little is wrong. Some senior people are not open to new ideas – [there can be] lots of cynicism. One interviewee observed that, 'the wrong leadership' [is often] in post too long and boards are reluctant to dismiss them'.

Some leaders fear losing control. There are still those who are schooled in the old way of thinking that when [they] the boss says jump, people [are supposed to say], 'how high? – but they have failed to realize that people are no longer prepared to work this way. Another respondent reported that there is 'evidence that many CEOs lack awareness and don't realize the impact of neglecting people and [ignoring] collaboration'. One interviewee observed that there are huge gaps in management education, with a significant bias still towards short-term and financial objectives.

The employees are not ready. Those who have worked Level 2 or Level 3 environments for a long time can be sceptical about change programmes led by senior management. They may have gone through earlier initiatives that were either poorly conceived or poorly executed. '[You may] need to overcome cynical employees, which can be debilitating for the authentic leader. Leaders need to work hard to give clarity and get positive feedback, but there still remains negative cynicism.'

One can come across an entitlement culture among some employees who are not inclined to give that extra effort to make Level 4 work. Others are more comfortable with a hierarchy and having someone to blame for everything that goes wrong. 'It is easy for a genuine authentic leader to lose trust – resilience is needed in the face of cynicism.

When putting in a new collaborative system, it can be difficult to achieve the balance between accountability and blame if people are immature. Another observation was, 'if it is not addressed at all layers, the presence of fear can prevent change.' In a jaded culture, words and phrases such as enthusiasm, leadership, unlimited passion etc. are open to ridicule rather than inspiration, and 'employees are brilliant at detecting a lack of authenticity.'

In some organizations, the leaders are ready and the junior staff willing, but there is a mid-tier section of people who, for a range of reasons, are not going to feel comfortable. Worse still, they feel threatened. If you can't get a compelling vision at the top, you will often not engage with the mid-levels.

The effort is perceived as too great. 'Change is tiring,' and 'too great a challenge,' for many people, with the result that some employees leave. Another comment was, 'If we're not strong and resilient we will not be able to drive the cultural change.' One interviewee observed, however, that change was, in fact, gradual and linear, not the *hockey-stick curve* they had expected.

> 'Many organizations, including the NHS, have a strong management culture in terms of values. However, their ability to deliver short-term results and stay on top of a short-term agenda when there are major societal changes, e.g. people living longer, new cures for diseases etc., has become increasingly difficult. We need to have a major rethink on how we manage these challenges.'

It's still perceived as not business-like. Despite the strong evidence chronicled throughout this and other books about the superior returns from Levels 4 and 5, there is a strong legacy and a cultural belief that focusing on the numbers and short-term results is more business-like. That is a cultural challenge that has no quick fix. There remains the concept of putting profits before people, forgetting that, ultimately, all profits come from the activity of your people.

Business is still seen by many as a factory for making money rather than as an organization that identifies problems, provides solutions and improves the quality of life. 'There's also a big challenge with the lack of external focus. People are too internally focussed, their only purpose is to make money or grow.' There remains also a cultural tendency to focus on the short-term only, but businesses have to continually earn the *permission* to operate and, as recent scandals have shown, they cannot take this for granted.

Those who benefit from the status quo may fear a loss of wealth or influence if radical change is introduced. One comment was, 'Most CEOs will, in their hearts, want to impact society positively. They don't want poverty, climate change etc., but the current economic climate makes it difficult.' Many managers still fail to see the benefits of volunteering or of accepting social responsibility.

Perception of work and life being separate. The mechanization of the business model into structures with resources is accompanied by a belief that one ought to be more ruthless and cynical in business than in other walks of life. Research for this book challenges this false demarcation, but it remains a difficult cultural barrier to overcome. One respondent observed, 'Many people still think that work and life must be separate, but they are not. Understanding the concept that we live by the same ethics and values for both is difficult for some.'

Table 7.2 shows the top twenty barriers to the *Big Shift* (expressed as a lack of the concepts listed). This was obtained from a NVivo analysis of all answers obtained on this topic from interviewees, as well as from the frequency of certain themes that were mentioned in the context of barriers. It is apparent that the top barriers to the *Big Shift* are related to the mindset and attitude, and motivation (of both leaders and employees).

Figure 7.2 shows a word cloud obtained from all of the quotes related to the barriers. People feature prominently in this image.

Arie de Geus identifies company law as one of the key barriers to the shift:

> I do believe that, just as with the French Revolution, we need a legal centre to really change the structure of the way [in which] power is acquired, the way power is exercised and the way that power is controlled. As long as company law is still pre-Napoleon and pre-French revolution, we won't see that massive *shift* because there will always be people who abuse: the *bruisers,* the *hairy alpha males* and some women as well.

While many barriers to the *Big Shift* and to humanizing organizations have been identified, one issue stands out as an enabler – creating employee-owned

TABLE 7.2 *Top twenty barriers to the* Big Shift *from N Vivo analysis*

Barriers to shifting	Total frequency
1. Mindset and attitude	108
2. Motivation of employees	100
3. Aligning of people and systems	66
4. Organizational learning processes	51
5. Practising people aspects of an organization	49
6. Opportunities for learning and development	40
7. Understanding strategic direction	39
8. Self-organization of employees in communities	39
9. Compensation schemes	37
10. Distribution of decision making	36
11. Alignment of individual and organizational values	35
12. Prioritizing long-term performance	35
13. Emotional intelligence	33
14. Collaborative development of strategy	32
15. Values	30
16. Talent retention	30
17. Skills of employees	27
18. Distribution of authority	27
19. Innovation embedded in strategy	24
20. Experimenting with new ideas	24

FIGURE 7.2 *Word cloud created from all of the quotes related to barriers to the Big Shift.*

organizations. Graeme Nuttall OBE, the UK Government adviser on employee ownership, stated that:

> It would be extremely unusual to find a command and control method of managing in an employee-owned company, unless it was vital for, say, health and safety reasons. In broad terms, employee-owned companies encourage constructive dissent. They want employees to share good ideas.

He added:

> In order to achieve employee ownership, you need good employee engagement as well as an ownership stake and financial participation. It is inherent in the ownership structure that the employees have a financial stake. I think that makes a tremendous difference to the attitudes of employees.

He argued that switching to employee ownership won't necessarily transform engagement in itself, but it can change the context significantly because everyone has a stake. Where there is no such stake and, instead, a manager returns from an external training course with some ideas for engagement and improvement, there can be scepticism. If the employees have a stake in the business, however, the incentive to be part of the new direction is considerably enhanced.

Utilizing power levers to create more humane workplaces

It would be easy to suppose that behaviours at Level 4 and 5, where passion and additional voluntary initiatives are clearly visible, are motivated exclusively by goodwill and that there are no power dynamics are at play. In fact, power is still a factor but it works in a very different way than at the lower levels. At Level 1, power is based on fear and little is achieved. At Level 2, power relies on an imbalance of information, which is all held by the senior management. Level 3 is more tolerable, but very unequal, with power often residing in the ego of a powerful individual. At Levels 4 and 5 there are transformational changes and there is a motivating force for improving the quality of life. Power is exerted on individuals to commit themselves and to contribute, but it is exercised through positive peer pressure and an enlightened sense of purpose. Positive ripples spread out from individuals to the group and from one group to another. It is not exercised through fear (Levels 1 and 2) or force of law (Level 3). Figure 7.3 shows the power levers mapped to the five Levels of the individual mindset.

Understanding this distinction can be helpful in overcoming some of the barriers discussed earlier in this chapter, and especially for managers schooled in Level 3 thinking. They are not giving up power and influence, they are enhancing it, but in a very different way.

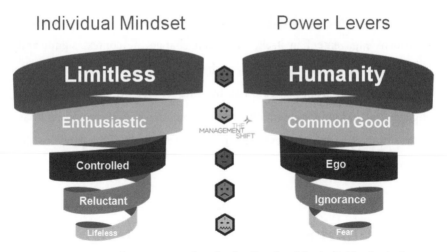

FIGURE 7.3 *Power levers mapped to the five Levels of the individual mindset.*

The impact of not taking action

Management and leadership, indeed all professional roles, involve making decisions. Earlier in this chapter I discussed some of the barriers to implementing the *Management Shift*. Some of them are easily understandable, some less so. Some are formidable, others can be overcome in a more straightforward way. With all such decisions, however, there is an impact.

We know from the evidence presented in this book that moving sustainably from Level 3 to Level 4 will lead to major improvements in social, psychological and financial indicators, but what is the impact of *not* acting? Deciding to stick with Level 3 is a choice and all choices have consequences. As part of the research for this book, I asked interviewees for their views on the consequences of not acting. In some cases, the examples are real – they moved to Level 4 and experienced the benefits. Here's what some of them said:

> I think the consequences of not *shifting* are an increased loss of productivity, loss of competitive advantage, continued inequality and a growth of inequality in society. There are consequences that range from the micro

level, e.g. a firm can be performing less well or imploding as we've seen with the very famous recent example of Tesco. There are also consequences at a macro level, e.g. the UK's reduction in its rate of productivity. There are consequences on a global level. There are consequences everywhere.

ANN FRANCKE

Overconsumption, environmental stress, climate change and the planets inherent capacity to support life is being exceeded. Too many people are being left behind. There are uneconomic levels of debt at both governmental and domestic level. If you do not take care of our finite resources, or if you run your companies irresponsibly from a human compliance point of view, you will be flushed out increasingly quickly by the transparency that younger organizations insist upon.

PAUL POLMAN

The autocratic approach, as you so rightly say in *The Management Shift*, just doesn't work and people leave in droves. Why do people leave a job, fundamentally? It's because of the boss, usually their immediate boss, but do they still trust in the leadership of the company?

MARTIN MACKAY

One big thing that I think is going to happen is that we're going to run out of talent, because a lot of talented young people don't want to work for an organization that's just there to churn out gadgets and make money. They want to do something that has a purpose.

NIGEL GIRLING

I think when you look at organizations that are run in the traditional fashion, they are in steep decline and the rate of return on assets is a quarter of what it was fifty years ago and the life expectancy [of companies] has reduced from seventy-five years to ten years. I mean, these are pretty worrying trends that are concealed by various financial engineering tricks.

The economy and these organizations are in real decline. It's not a question of whether, it's a question of when.

STEVE DENNING

I think we probably would have gone out of business [if we hadn't made *the Management Shift*]. Recruitment businesses are very sensitive to a downturn in the economy.

SIMON LA FOSSE

I think the organization would never have had been able to achieve these great scores in customer satisfaction, profitability and continuity without *The Management Shift*, because we would just be another mediocre-quality IT company. Also, I do not believe that we would have been able to attract the talent we now have.

GERWIN SCHURING

If this doesn't happen, if we cannot find ways of becoming more productive as a society, we will lose our way economically. The wealth that currently supports a very civilized society in terms of the arts, the quality of our broadcasting systems, the sport we excel at, the science that we're famous for and all those civilized behaviours that depend upon a prosperous, efficient and productive society will also be in jeopardy.

JULES GODDARD

Doing well by doing good: the next steps

We can all create and spread ripples through our thoughts and actions. Every change starts with a single step in the right direction and, with everything that is going on in the business and political world, the question remains, 'If we do not start taking action toward a *Big Shift* that humanizes organizations, a shift that will lead to an improvement in performance and profit as well as creating more purposeful lives, when are we going to do it?' Will we get another chance to create a better future for the younger generation?

There are practical steps that we can take, so it is not an unrealistic goal. Arie de Geus said, 'Well if people would read your book, absorb it, and then decide to apply it – even the *hairy alpha male* – it will all happen automatically because it works. We know it works.'

David Macleod reports that some executives still shy away from opening up or showing their vulnerability. Hence it is important to make both a rational and a business case. 'What we need to do is to convince more chief executives that by being an engaging leader and by acknowledging that the people who come to work for us are human beings, we set out working conditions that are much more likely to create success.'

Richard Barrett adds: 'if you just keep on doing what you're doing, you should recognize that you'll never reach fulfilment until you become engaged. Some people are able to do that, others are not. The ones who don't get stressed out trying to control everything, but instead allow people to express themselves and give them the space to find fulfilment in their lives – and I'm talking employees here – will make their company more successful. That's really what it's all about.'

Stephen Denning warns that the consequences of having a 'business as usual approach' are dire. 'Get started! It's a journey one is going to have to make sooner or later. The sooner one learns about it, the sooner one gets started on it and the sooner one makes progress. None of these organizations have just arrived, they are all on a continuing journey in which they continue to reinvent themselves and continue to inspect, adapt and change. It's more important to get started on the move to change rather than thinking that it's a finite journey from A to B. It's from A to B to C to D and onwards.'

Concluding thoughts

The work presented in this book, and in my previous books and publications, is driven by my life purpose and mission to help to *shift* the world of business so that it becomes more humanized, while creating high-performing ways of working that will make this world a better place. In addition to my writing and speaking, I have created online tools and educational material that is used by many organizations worldwide to achieve the *Management Shift* to Level 4 through the activities of *The Management Shift Consulting Ltd.* I have provided an overview of the resources available, which can be found in Figure 7.4, while Appendix 6 provides additional information about these activities and tools.

People are at the centre of both value creation and creating value for customers. Many companies pursue numbers and neglect people – they focus on the right side of the *6 Box Leadership Model* and neglect the left side. They will not be able to achieve sustained performance and profit on a long-term basis.

If they choose to chase quarterly profits and an increase in the share price in the short-term, they neglect the culture and the way people learn and develop within their company. If their people are burnt out, unhappy, disengaged, no longer passionate and their voice is not being heard, performance will stagnate.

My hypothesis, strongly borne out by the case studies in this book and in my previous publications, is that when organizations pay attention to the left side of the model, when they nurture people and put in place processes and incentives that allow people to unleash their creativity, people then have a passion for their work. They see what their purpose is and they're connected to the company's higher purpose. After that, the numbers take care of themselves.

The collective wisdom of those leaders interviewed for this book, who have over 1,700 years cumulative experience, supports this hypothesis. As well as

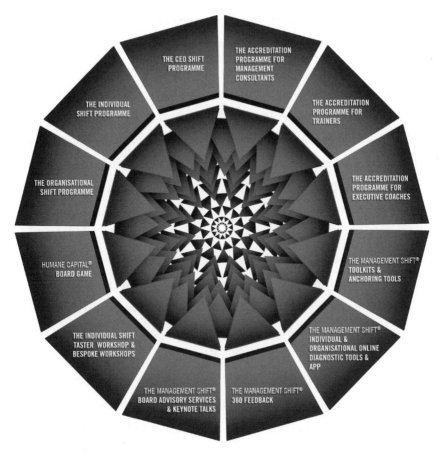

FIGURE 7.4 *Resources available to help* The Management Shift *(see also Appendix 6).*

many other research studies, including the extensive research presented in my previous book, *The Management Shift*, the case for the *Big Shift* is so compelling that it is only a question of when, not if, developing *humane capital* will prevail in the majority of organizations.

As Curtis Carlson said:

If people don't treat each other with respect, is excellent performance going to happen? No. If people don't have integrity, is it going to happen? No. Because of the rapid progress and challenges of the global innovation economy, positive human values are even more important today than they were twenty years ago. The faster things go, the more important human interactions become.

One issue is that all the hard problems that have to be solved today are multi-disciplinary in nature and they require multi-disciplinary teams. That's a challenge because different disciplines speak different languages, they have different perspectives and they have different business models. You need people to come together and I would argue that you need to train them, but if you don't emphasize human values at the same time they will not work together. They just won't. However, if you can tap into the core human motivators, the advantage to the organization is tremendous.

People sometimes look at the downside and say, 'Oh, it's too soft, it's not going to be effective enough,' but the truth is if you can get people to collaborate intensely you're looking at improvements of hundreds of per cent. Not ten per cent, it's hundreds of per cent.

SRI is a perfect example of that. How does an organization with 1,200 people (when I got there), that was effectively bankrupt and had no money (over my ten years as CEO there), triple in size and create $50 billion of new economic value. It is now considered by some to be the most productive pound-for-pound R&D organization in the world. That's because we got our people to work together intensely on these big, important problems. We used value-creation playbooks and value creation forums to learn to collaborate positively and productively. You have to treat people with respect, they have to become engaged, you have to motivate them and you have to ensure that the organization is transparent. If those things become broken the learning stops, and it is the learning that allows you to go from a failing proposition to creating a huge amount of new value.

The challenge here is to design the organization so that it makes all of these results inevitable. If the structures don't drive these activities or behaviours, then they go away quickly or they will be seen as too difficult.

That is what we did. We created an architecture that ensured that the behaviours, learning and results we wanted became inevitable.

The time for taking action is now!

Working on this book has been a wonderful experience with so many insights, eureka moments and challenges. *When we have gone through the storm, we enjoy stillness more. When we meet our vulnerability, we realise how strong we are. When we experience authoritarianism, we develop more compassion. When we experience darkness, we appreciate light more.*

In humanized organizations we embrace our strengths, we are compassionate, resilient and purposeful. We unleash the power of human spirit with a passion to make this world a better place while working on something far greater than we are. As many interviewees said, this is a choice between happiness and a wasted life, between surviving and thriving, between life and death. We can all make a difference and we can all create ripples. If we don't do it now, then when shall we do it? The time is now!

 SEVEN REFLECTION POINTS FROM THIS CHAPTER

1 Are you aware of your daily influence on the people around you?
2 Do you see the connections between the individual and the group, and their performance? Do you see that the barriers to the *Management Shift* may be personal and/or collective, and at different levels of seniority?
3 Do you pay attention to mindsets as well as systems and training? Do you challenge the cynical view that regards people as being resources or cost units?
4 In a world where the autocratic leadership model is increasingly being rejected, does your organization have a single leader with high levels of power?

5 Is the initiative to adopt the *Management Shift* motivated solely by your concerns for welfare, or do you recognize the importance of resilience and organizational success?

6 To what extent do you and your organization consider the wider impact you have on society and the environment?

7 Are you making immediate plans to move towards a highly-engaged, high-performing workplace, or is this a project that tends to be postponed?

APPENDIX 1. INTERVIEW QUESTIONS

1   Would you like to tell us a bit about your background?

2   Are you familiar with the concepts described in *The Management Shift* book?

3   Did your organization go through a *shift* from Level 3 to Level 4, as described in this book?

   a   What problems were you facing?

   b   What have you done to try to solve those problems?

   c   Why did those solutions fail?

4   How did you measure and monitor the impacts of *the shift*?

5   What were the effects, both organizationally and financially?

6   What do you think would have happened if you did not go through *the shift*?

7   What did your organization do to make this *shift* happen?

8   How do you see your organization now? What is your world outlook now?

9   If you could buy this result, what price tag would it have?

10 Would you recommend that others go through the *shift*? Why would you recommend it?

11 If you look at other companies, which of them are going through the *shift* and why?

12 Are you aware of those companies that have implemented a Level 4
    (people and purpose-based) leadership?

13 Are there any final comments you would like to make? What advice
    would you give to others considering going through the shift?

APPENDIX 2. LIST OF INTERVIEWEES

(listed in the order of interviews)

NAME	POSITION (at the time of interview)	TOPIC	SECTOR/ INDUSTRY
Chris Shern	Former General Manager, Scandinavian Airlines; CEO of Henley Business School Scandinavia, **Denmark**	Individual *shift* story, expert view	Public sector/ Education
Doug Kirkpatrick	Consultant to The Morning Star Company, **USA**	Management at Morning Star	Private sector/ Manufacturing
Kevin O'Brien	Former Application Engineer at WL Gore & Associates, **USA**	Management at WL Gore	Private sector/ Manufacturing
Jack Bergstrand	CEO of Brand Velocity Inc; Former CIO and CFO for Coca Cola Corporation Inc., **USA**	Organizational *shift* at Brand Velocity	Private sector/ Management consulting
Marshall Goldsmith	One of the Top Ten Most-influential Business Thinkers in the World, **USA**	Expert view on the *shift* to inspirational leadership	Private sector/ Management consulting
Celine Shillinger	Head of Quality, Innovation & Engagement at Sanofi Pasteur, **USA**	The power of networks/role of technology, Sanofi Pasteur Case Study,	Private sector/ Pharmaceutical
Peter Cheese	CEO of the Chartered Institute for Personnel Development, **UK**	CIPD perspective on the *shift* to inspirational leadership	Non-profit/ Professional association

Ann Francke	CEO of the Chartered Management Institute, **UK**	CIM perspective on the *shift* to inspirational leadership	Non-profit/ Professional association
Richard Barrett	Chairman of Barrett's Values Centre, **UK**	*Shift* to values based inspirational leadership	Private sector/ Management consulting
Vineet Nayar	Former CEO of HCL Technologies, **India**	*Shift* at HCL Technologies	Private sector/IT consulting
Anders Bouvin	CEO, Handelsbanken, **UK/Sweden**	Case study Handelsbanken, **UK/Sweden**	Private sector/ Banking
Avivah Wittenberg-Cox	CEO of 20-First, **UK**	Gender balance and the *shift* to inspirational leadership	Private sector/ Management consulting
Ry Morgan	CEO of Yomp, **UK**	Millennials and the *shift* to inspirational leadership	Private sector/ Services
Mick Yates	Former Company Group Chairman, Johnson and Johnson; Vice President Procter and Gamble, **UK**	Expert view on the *shift*, an example of the shift at Johnson and Johnson	Private sector/ Manufacturing
Steven Denning	Author; former Programme Director at World Bank, **USA**	Expert view on the *shift* to inspirational leadership	Private sector/ Management consulting
Sir Paul Judge	Chairman of AMBA, CMI and the Schroeder Investment trust, **UK**	Expert view on the *shift* to inspirational leadership at Cadbury	Private/Public sector/ Education/ Services
Dana Denis-Smith	CEO of Obelisk Ltd	Gender balance, new ways of working, Obelisk case study, **UK**	Private sector/ Legal services

Rob Noble	CEO of The Leadership Trust, **UK**	Expert view on the *shift* to inspirational leadership	Non-profit/ Education
Paul Polman	CEO of Unilever, **UK/the Netherlands**	Building purpose focused organizations (Unilever), a CEO perspective	Private sector/ Manufacturing
Geoff McDonald	Former HR President for Unilever, **UK**	Building purpose focused organizations – a HR perspective on building purpose and focused alliance *shifts* at Unilever	Private sector/ Management consulting/ Manufacturing
Charlie Isaacs	CTO of Salesforce, **USA**	Inspirational leadership case study, Salesforce	Private sector/IT
John Stepper	MD of Deutsche Bank, **USA**	Expert view on the *shift*, Working out loud concept, DB case study	Private sector/ Banking
Paul Excell	Former Chief Innovation Officer for BT, **UK**	Innovation and the *shift* to inspirational leadership	Private sector/ Management consulting/IT
Rob Wirszycz	Former Director General of Intellect; Chairman of several IT companies, **UK**	Role of technology for the *shift* to inspirational leadership	Private sector/ Management consulting/ IT
Charles Elvin	CEO of the Institute of Leadership and Management, **UK**	ILM perspective on the *shift* to inspirational leadership	Private sector/ Education
Graeme Nuttall OBE	UK Government adviser on employee ownership, **UK**	Influence of employee ownership on management practices	Public sector/UK Government

Martin Donnelly	Permanent Secretary at Department for Business, Innovation and Skills, **UK**	Government perspective on diversity and management; gender balance in BIS, BIS case study	Public sector/UK Government
Simon Fowler	The John Lewis Partnership, Partnership Registrar; John Lewis Board, **UK**	Employee ownership and management practices, John Lewis case study	Private sector/ Employee owned/Retail
Martin Mackay	CEO, Experior Group, **UK**	Organizational *shift* in the Experior Group	Private sector/IT consulting
Michael Goethe	CEO/Founder, CRISP Consultancy, **Sweden**	Self-management case study, CRISP Consultancy	Private sector/ Management consulting
Paul Dolman and Helen Walton	CEO/Marketing Director, Gamevy Ltd, **UK**	Self-management, agile case study, Gamevy Ltd	Private sector/ Employee owned/IT
Stelio Verzera	Founder, Liquid Organisation, **Italy**	Collaboration and self-management case study, Liquid Organisation	Private sector/ Management consulting
Jack Hubbard	CEO, Propellernet, **UK/ France**	Self-management – case study, Propellernet	Private sector/ Media and PR
Nigel Girling	CEO, National Centre for Strategic Leadership, **UK**	Expert view on the *shift* to inspirational leadership	Public sector/ Education
Jules Goddard	Senior Fellow, London Business School, **UK**	Expert view on the *shift* to inspirational leadership	Public sector/ Education

Jos de Blok	CEO, Buurtzorg, **the Netherlands**	The *shift* in healthcare, self-management cases study in Buurtzorg	Private sector/ Health services
Simon La Fosse	CEO, La Fosse Associates, **UK**	The *shift* in executive recruitment, case study at La Fosse Associates	Private sector/ Recruitment agency
David MacLeod OBE	Co-leader on the UK government task force on engagement, **UK**	Expert view on the *shift*, engagement	Public sector/UK government
Dame Fiona Woolf CBE	Former Lord Major of the City of London, **UK**	Expert view on the *shift*, gender balance	Public sector/UK government/ Private sector/ Legal services
Brian Walker	CEO of Herman Miller, **USA**	Herman Miller case study	Public sector/ Design
Tom Rippin	CEO of On Purpose, **UK**	On Purpose case study	Non-profit/ Education
Anita Krohn Traaseth	CEO of Innovasjon Norway; Former CEO of HP Norway, **Norway**	Management *shift* in Innovation Norway	Public sector/ Norwegian government
Paul Little	CEO and Principal of the City of Glasgow College, **UK**	*Management shift* in the City of Glasgow College	Public sector/ Education
Rick Wartzman	Executive Director of the Drucker institute, **USA**	Expert view on the *shift* to inspirational leadership	Non-profit/ Education/ Management consulting
Gerwin Schuring	CEO Schuberg Philis, **the Netherlands**	Self-management, A case study, Schuberg Philis	Private sector/ Security technology
Richard Straub	President of the Drucker Society Europe, **Austria**	Expert view on the *shift* to a new management paradigm	Non-profit/Event management/ Education

Arie de Geus	Former Director of Strategy at Royal Dutch Shell plc, **UK**	Expert view on the *shift* to inspirational leadership	Private sector/Oil industry
Karin Tenelius	CEO, Tuff Ledarskapsträning, **Sweden**	Expert view on the *shift* to inspirational leadership	Private sector/ Management consulting
Stephen Ball	CEO, Lockheed Martin, **UK**	Lockheed Martin, case study	Private sector/ Manufacturing
Lord David Evans	Chairman, Institute of Collaborative Working, **UK**	ICW, Senate Publishing case study	Private sector/ Publishing
Caroline Minshell	CEO, Senate Publishing, **UK**	Senate Publishing case study	Private sector/ Publishing
Justin Packshaw	CEO De Roemer/ Explorer, **UK**	Expert view on the *shift* to inspirational leadership	Private sector/ Luxury fashion/ Exploring expeditions
Ajaz Ahmed Sam Kelly	CEO/MD AKQA, **UK**	AKQA case study	Private sector/ Innovative industries
Kalyan Madabhushi	General Manager, Royal Dutch Shell, **the Netherlands**	Royal Dutch Shell, group case study	Private sector/Oil industry
Curtis Carlson	Former President and CEP of the Stanford Research Institute (SRI) International, **USA**	RSI International, Case Study	Private sector/ Innovation
Michael Jenkins	CEO of Roffey Park Leadership Institute, **UK**	Roffey Park case study	Non-profit sector

APPENDIX 3. DEMOGRAPHIC DATA FOR INTERVIEWEES AND THEIR ORGANIZATIONS

A3.1 Location of Interviewees

Location of Interviewees	Count
UK	34
USA	11
the Netherlands	3
Sweden	2
Austria	1
Denmark	1
Italy	1
India	1
Norway	1
UK/France	1
UK/the Netherlands	1
UK/Sweden	1
Total	58

A3.2 Interviewees by position and gender

	Male	Female
Author	1	
Board Member	1	
CEO	23	6
Chairman	4	
Co-Leader, Government Task Force	1	
Consultant	1	
CTO	1	
Executive Director	1	
Former Application Engineer	1	
Former CEO	1	1
Former Chief Innovation Officer	1	
Former CIO and CFO	1	
Former Company Group Chairman	1	
Former Director of Strategy	1	
Former Director General	1	
Former General Manager	1	
Former HR President	1	
Former Lord Mayor		1
Former President and CEP	1	
Former Program Director	1	
Founder	2	
General Manager	1	
Government Advisor	1	

Head of Quality, Innovation and Engagement	1	
Influential Business Thinker	1	
Marketing Director		1
MD	1	
Permanent Secretary	1	
President	1	
Principal	1	
Senior Fellow	1	
Vice President	1	

A3.3 Interviewees' organization names and location

Organisation	Location
20-First	UK
AMBA	UK
AKQA	UK
Barrett's Value Centre	UK
BIS	UK
Brand Velocity Inc.	USA
BT	UK
Buurtzorg	the Netherlands
CIPD (Chartered Institute for Personnel Development)	UK
City of Glasgow College	UK
City of London	UK
CMI (Chartered Management Institute)	UK
CRISP	Sweden
Deutsche Bank	USA
De Roemer / Explorer	UK
Drucker Institute	USA
Drucker Society Europe	Austria
Experior Group	UK
Gamevy	UK
Handelsbanken	Sweden/UK
HCL Technologies	India
Henley Business School	UK

Henley Business School (Scandinavia)	Denmark
Herman Miller	USA
ILM	UK
Innovasjon Norway	Norway
Institute of Collaborative Working	UK
Institute of Leadership and Management	UK
Intellect	UK
John Lewis Partnership	UK
La Fosse Associates	UK
Liquid Organisation	Italy
Lockheed Martin	UK
London Business School	UK
Morning Star	USA
National Centre for Strategic Leadership	UK
Obelisk Ltd.	UK
On Purpose	UK
Procter and Gamble	UK
Propellernet	UK/France
Roffey Park Leadership Institute	UK
Royal Dutch Shell	UK
Salesforce	USA
Sanofi Pasteur	USA
Schroeder Investment Trust	UK
Schuberg Philis	the Netherlands
Senate Publishing	UK

Stanford Research Institute (SRI) International	USA
The Leadership Trust	UK
Tuff Ledarskapstraning	Sweden
UK Government	UK
Unilever	UK/the Netherlands
W L Gore & Associates	USA
World Bank	USA
Yomp	UK

A3.4 Interviewees by Sector and Industry

	Private (Corporates and SMEs)	Public	Non-profit
Banking	1		
Banking – Employee Owned	1		
Design		1	
Education	2	4	4
Event Management			1
Health Services	1		
Innovative Industries	2		
IT	3		
IT Consulting	2		
IT-Employee owned	1		
Legal Services	2		
Luxury Fashion/Travel	1		
Management Consulting	11		1
Management Education			1
Manufacturing	6		
Media & PR	1		
Norwegian Government		1	
Oil Industry	2		
Pharmaceutical	1		
Professional Association			2
Publishing	2		
Recruitment Agency	1		

Retail – Employee Owned	1	
Security Technology	1	
Services	1	1
UK Government		4

APPENDIX 4. RESEARCH METHODOLOGY UNDERPINNING THE *HUMANE CAPITAL* PROJECT

The qualitative research presented in this book was conducted over a period of eighteen months. A total of fifty-eight organizational leaders were interviewed by the author using a semi-structured interview approach[1]. All of the interviews were recorded and transcribed, and all transcripts were approved by interviewees before they were used for data analysis. Data was analysed both manually, using thematic analysis, and by using qualitative data analysis software, NVivo, version 11.4.0.

A4.1 Thematic analysis

Following the approval of written transcripts by interviewees, an exploratory (content driven) thematic analysis with coding was conducted.[2] Coding is a way of indexing or categorizing the text in order to establish a framework of thematic ideas about it.[3] Thematic analysis is often used in qualitative research for examining themes within data and, as I had to deal with large data sets and was searching for categories to emerge from that data, I judged that it was the most suitable research method[4] to combine thematic analysis with data analysis using NVivo software. Qualitative data analysis involves the analysis of text, pictures or sounds but, in this case, the data was largely in text form.

Six phases of thematic analysis[5] were followed in this research:

- *Phase 1: Familiarization with the data.* This involved reading and re-reading interview transcripts (overall these transcripts extended to more than 272,000 words), highlighting the most relevant parts using different colour codes, note-taking and creating a list of initial codes.

- *Phase 2: Generating initial codes.* In this phase the initial codes were generated and the lists of the sources of patterns were produced in table formats. Data was collapsed into labels to create categories, and inferences about the meaning of codes were made.

- *Phase 3: Searching for themes.* This involved combining codes into overarching themes and producing a list of themes for further analysis.

- *Phase 4: Reviewing themes.* In this phase themes were analyzed to determine how they supported the data.

- *Phase 5: Defining and naming themes.* Each theme was defined and described, with an analysis as to how these themes supported the data.

- *Phase 6: Producing the report.* In this phase a description of the results was produced.

A4.2 Data analysis using qualitative data analysis software NVivo

In addition to the manual thematic analysis of data, interview transcripts were analyzed using the qualitative data analysis software, NVivo. Transcripts were uploaded with the attributes (meta-data) for each interviewee assigned, which included their gender, sector, industry and location. Combinations of this meta-data contributed to the creation of various tables relating to the demographic data relative to interviewees. The next step was to then code and analyze the transcripts themselves. On the first reading of each interview transcript, relevant sections of text were highlighted and coded against broad themes (nodes) that were initially aligned to the interview structure:

1 Why did they need to go through The *Big Shift* to Level 4?

2 What did they change?

3 How did they change?

4 What was the outcome of *shifting?*

5 What were the barriers to *shifting?*

6 What was the estimated impact of not *shifting?*

7 What was the 'price tag' (value) of the *Big Shift?*

8 Examples given of Level 4 companies, as indicated by the interviewees.

Each section of highlighted (coded) text created a unique reference with the frequency of these individual references forming data tables, created using the 6 Box Leadership Model[6] themes as a framework for analysis. Sets of references were also exported to Word documents for further review and analysis as required.

To be able to explore the data in more detail, the individual items that contribute to each of the 6 Box Leadership Model themes were also specifically coded, for example:

1 **C09**: Trust (Culture theme)

2 **REL01**: Collaboration (Relationships theme)

3 **IN05**: Motivation of employees (Individuals theme)

4 **SY02**: Distribution of authority (Systems theme)

5 **ST04**: Understanding of strategic direction (Strategy theme)

6 **RS07**: IT Infrastructure (Resources theme)

The next step was to review the extracts again and code from the perspective of each of the 6 Box Leadership Model themes: the people-related aspects

(Culture, Relationships and Individuals) and the process-related aspects (Strategy, Systems and Resources). This was done for the references relating to the following themes used in interview questions:

1   Why did they need to change?

2   What did they change?

3   How did they change?

4   What were the barriers to *shifting*?

5   What was the impact of not *shifting*?

In order to gain a different perspective and more insight into the process of the 'What or how did they change?' question, these specific references were also reviewed and coded against four further themes:

1   Helping others to *shift*

2   Personal (individual) *shift*

3   Process themes

4   Purpose themes

The detailed codes (e.g. C09) for individual 6 Box Leadership Model items provided the data for the full listing and summary tables for queries such as: 'How to *shift*' (an aggregate of all the 'How' themes), 'Helping others *shift*', 'Processes for *shifting*', 'How to make a personal *shift*' and 'Barriers to *shifting*'.

Extracts of the 'Why did they change', coded by the 6 Box Leadership Model themes, were reviewed as Word documents, but not specifically analysed using NVivo software.

Finally, the 'price tag' (the value of the *shift*) references were coded against three broad perspectives: business, personal and global benefits. The Level 4 companies suggested by the interviewees were independently collated.

A4.3 Research stages used

Table A4.1 shows a summary of the key research stages undertaken in this project, the procedures used and the key outcomes of each stage.

TABLE A4.1 *Research stages used in data collection and analysis*

Research Stage	Procedure	Product/Outcome
Development of questions for semi-structured interviews	• Iterative development of questions for semi-structured interviews • Piloting the list of questions with five professionals	• Final list of questions used for semi-structured interviews with leaders
Data collection: semi-structured interviews	• Individual face-to-face, Skype or phone interviews with fifty-eight leaders • Email follow up for the approval of the transcripts	• Audio data (interview recordings) • Text data (interview transcripts with over 272,000 words in transcripts)
Qualitative data analysis	• Coding key data using NVivo software • Manual coding of data in case studies into four sectors (corporate, public sector, SMEs and non-profit sector), data related to barriers to the *shift*, value of the *shift* etc.	• Codes and themes for aggregate data • Key strategies for humanizing organizations in each sector, key barriers to the *shift*, value of the *shift* etc.
Interpretation of data	• Interpretation and explanation of data	• Discussions • Development of frameworks with strategies and key themes

APPENDIX 5. LEVEL 4 COMPANIES IDENTIFIED BY INTERVIEWEES

Company	Country	Industry
1. Amazon	UK/USA	Retail
2. Apple	USA	Technology
3. Basecamp	USA	Web technology
4. Borrow My Doggy	UK	Pet sitter
5. Buurtzorg	the Netherlands	Healthcare
6. C.H. Robinson	UK	Logistics and supply chain
7. Circle Holdings PLC	UK	Investment
8. Costco	USA	Wholesale and retail
9. Danone	France/Spain	Food products
10. Disney	USA	Media and entertainment
11. EA Gibson Shipbrokers	UK	Shipbrokers
12. Ericsson	Sweden	Network and telecommunications
13. Fairmount Minerals	USA	Mining
14. Flourish & Prosper (Global Forum for business)	UK	Wine merchant and delicatessen
15. GCHQ	UK	Intelligence and security
16. GlobeScan	Canada	Research consultancy
17. Google	USA	Technology

18. Grant Thornton	UK/USA	Accounting
19. Great Britain Cycling Team (Dave Brailsford)	UK	Sport
20. Gripple (Hugh Facey)	UK	Wire joining and tensioning systems
21. Hamleys	UK	Toys
22. Happy Computers (Henry Stewart)	UK	Training providers
23. Harley Davidson	US/UK	Motorcycles
24. Herman Miller	UK	Furniture design
25. Hiut	UK	Denim products
26. IKEA	Sweden	Furniture and home sales
27. Interface – tbc	USA	Carpets
28. John Lewis Partnership	UK	Retail
29. Kingfisher	UK	Home improvements
30. Loomio	New Zealand	Decision making software
31. M&S	UK	Retail
32. Magna International	Canada	Automotive supplier
33. Mary Knowles Homecare Partnership	UK	Care provider
34. Microsoft – the visual studio division	USA	Technology
35. MJP Architects	UK	Architects
36. Mondragon Cooperatives	Spain	Cooperatives
37. Morning Star	USA	Investment research and management
38. Nestle	USA/UK	Nutrition, health and wellness
39. Netflix	USA	Media and video

40. NHS – National Clinical Director for England (Alistair Burns)	UK	Health
41. Nike	USA	Sports
42. Patagonia	USA	Outdoor clothing

APPENDIX 6. *THE MANAGEMENT SHIFT CONSULTING LTD* SERVICES AND TOOLS

The Management Shift Consulting Ltd, a management consultancy and leadership development company, was established by Professor Hlupic in 2015 to help individuals and organizations *shift* to a higher level of performance, fulfilment and profit. The ultimate aim is to help individuals and organizations to do well by doing good. Vlatka and her team of strategic advisors, coaches, psychologists and change management specialists are spreading *The Management Shift*® ripples globally, using the following services and tools that have been applied by dozens of organizations worldwide.

The CEO Shift Programme

This is an exclusive six-week long leadership development programme for CEOs that is based on one-to-one coaching, individual and organizational diagnostics, and *The Management Shift*® *360 Feedback* data collection and analysis. It is designed to help CEOs to achieve an individual *shift* in mindset.

The Management Shift® 360 Feedback

This 360 Degrees Feedback tool was designed to assess each CEOs leadership style before and after The CEO Shift Programme.

The Individual Shift Programme

This three-month long programme is designed to *shift* senior leadership teams to embrace emerging leadership styles (*shifting* to a Level 4 mind-set). It consists of pre and post-assessments for leaders, three one-day workshops, self-directed learning and peer learning, and four one-to-one coaching sessions with The Management Shift Consulting Ltd coaching team. This support ensures that individual action plans are developed and deployed successfully.

The Individual Shift taster workshop and bespoke workshops

This includes a half-day *taster* workshop on *The Individual Shift* and individual diagnostics for a group of senior leaders in the organization.

The Organizational Shift Programme

This programme is designed to help organizations *shift* their organizational culture and become more focused on people and purpose. As a result, they can achieve an increase in engagement, performance, innovation and profitability. This is designed to be a unique programme specific to each organization and typically involves the *Management Shift* consulting team working with a client over a twelve-month period. Tools, bespoke techniques and the power of the client organization's people are utilized to shift the organization to a new level of performance.

Accreditation Programs for Management Consultants

The Management Shift Consulting Ltd train and accredit management consultants to use *The Management Shift®* material, tools and processes with their clients in order to achieve a *shift* in performance.

Accreditation Programs for Trainers

The Management Shift Consulting Ltd train and accredit trainers to use *The Management Shift®* material, tools and processes for their executive education programs.

Accreditation Programmes for Executive Coaches

The Management Shift Consulting Ltd train and accredit executive coaches to use *The Management Shift®* material, tools and processes for their coaching clients.

The Management Shift® Board Advisory services

The Management Shift Consulting Ltd team provide advice to boards of directors and investors on the specific management of mergers and acquisitions, collaborative partnerships, potential acquisitions or joint ventures, and auditing and assessing risk exposure in organizations. Using *The Management Shift®* approaches for these requirements can enhance the likelihood of a successful investment, divestment or acquisition based on the use of robust scientific methodologies and evidence-based due diligence consulting and advice.

The Management Shift® Toolkit and Anchoring Tools

An online *toolkit* with more than fifty items is available for use by clients. It has been developed by *The Management Shift Consulting Ltd* team and by *The Management Shift®* accredited management consultants and trainers. The Toolkit includes board games, posters, handouts, cards and masks, all of which have been created to help individuals and organizations go through the *shift* to a Level 4 mindset and culture.

Psychological anchoring tools are also available to help anchor the mindset at Level 4. They include mugs, coasters, mouse pads, key rings, place mats and T-shifts with Level 4 and 5 symbols that have inspirational messages on them designed to help anchor the thinking patterns at Level 4.

The Management Shift® Executive Coaching

Management Shift Consulting Ltd offer highly specialized individual and executive coaching services. We facilitate the individual *shift* in mindset using a variety of leading edge coaching methods and tools, which include the tools and processes used by Professor Hlupic and her team in their research and their extensive practical experience in working with C-level executives.

The Management Shift® Individual and Organisational Diagnostic Tools and App

Management Shift Consulting Ltd offer online individual and organizational diagnostic tools that are used for assessment as part of *The CEO Shift*, *The Individual Shift* and *The Organizational Shift* programmes. *The Management Shift®* App is also available to test some of these diagnostic tools.

Keynote talks

Vlatka gives keynote talks globally at corporate or public events where she shares her knowledge and experience, and spreads the ripples that will make this world a better place.

Humane Capital® Board Game

The Humane Capital® board game was developed to help organisations put ideas from this book into practice. Details are available at: http://www.themanagementshift.com/humane-capital-book-2/

NOTES

Chapter 1

1   Hlupic V. (2014) *The Management Shift – How to Harness the Power of People and Transform Your Organisation for Sustainable Success*, Palgrave Macmillan

2   Passion at Work: Cultivating worker passion as a cornerstone of talent development, *Deloitte University Press* 2014 http://dupress.com/articles/worker-passion-employee-behavior/?id=us:2el:3dc:dup825:eng:tmt

3   State of the Global Workplace, *Gallup*, October 2013 http://www.gallup.com/poll/165269/worldwide-employees-engaged-work.aspx

4   The 2015 Workforce Purpose Index, https://www.imperative.com/index

5   Nathan Bennett and G James Lemoine See, for example, What VUCA Really Means for You, *Harvard Business Review*, Jan-Feb 2014 https://hbr.org/2014/01/what-vuca-really-means-for-you Accessed 8 Feb 2016

6   https://www.bcg.com/publications/2015/strategy-die-another-day-what-leaders-can-do-about-the-shrinking-life-expectancy-of-corporations.aspx

7   Daniel Goleman and Richard E Boyatzis, Social Intelligence and the Biology of Leadership, *Harvard Business Review*, September 2008

8   Everything you Need to Know about your Millennial Co-workers, *Fortune* 23 June 2015 http://fortune.com/2015/06/23/know-your-millennial-co-workers/

9   *Management 2020:* Leadership to unlock long-term growth. Report by the UK Parliamentary Commission on the Future of Management and Leadership, July 2014, published by the *Chartered Management Institute*

10 Tom Goodwin, The Battle is for the Customer Interface, *TechCrunch*, 3 March 2015 http://techcrunch.com/2015/03/03/in-the-age-of-disintermediation-the-battle-is-all-for-the-customer-interface/#.nkkwx9w:0sCd

11 Adult Fiction eBooks outsold Hardbacks in 2011, *Huffington Post*, 18 July 2012 http://www.huffingtonpost.com/2012/07/18/book-statistics–2011_n_1684473.html

12 Kindle sales have disappeared says UK's largest book retailer, *Telegraph*, 6 January 2015 http://www.telegraph.co.uk/finance/newsbysector/retailandconsumer/11328570/Kindle-sales-have-disappeared-says-UKs-largest-book-retailer.html

13 Richard D'Aveni, The 3-D Printing Revolution, May 2015 *Harvard Business Review* https://hbr.org/2015/05/the–3-d-printing-revolution

14 Matthias Holweg, The Limits of 3D Printing, *Harvard Business Review* 23 June 2015 https://hbr.org/2015/06/the-limits-of–3d-printing

15 Groupthink Caused the Market to Fail, *Huffington Post Business* 25 May 2011 http://www.huffingtonpost.com/stan-sorscher/group-think-caused-the-ma_b_604810.html. See also, Matthew Hancock and Nadhim Zahawi (2011) *Masters of Nothing: How the crash will happen again unless we understand human nature*, Biteback Publishing

16 Katherine W Phillips, How Diversity Makes us Smarter, *Scientific American* 1 October 2014 http://www.scientificamerican.com/article/how-diversity-makes-us-smarter/

17 What Norway can Teach the US About Getting More Women into Boardrooms, *The Atlantic*, 4 May 2015 http://www.theatlantic.com/business/archive/2015/05/what-norway-can-teach-the-us-about-getting-more-women-into-boardrooms/392195/

18 Improving the gender balance on British Boards, 5-Year Summary (Davies review), October 2015 https://www.gov.uk/government/uploads/system/uploads/attachment_data/file/482059/BIS–15–585-women-on-boards-davies-review–5-year-summary-october–2015.pdf

Chapter 2

1 Hlupic V. (2014) *The Management Shift – How to Harness the Power of People and Transform Your Organisation for Sustainable Success*, Palgrave Macmillan

2 King A. and Crewe I. (2013) *The Blunders of our Governments*, Oneworld Publications.

Chapter 3

1 https://www.virgin.com/unite/100-human-work

Chapter 5

1 https://www.drucker.institute/

2 http://engageforsuccess.org/engaging-for-success

Chapter 6

1 Hlupic V. (2014) *The Management Shift – How to Harness the Power of People and Transform Your Organisation for Sustainable Success*, Palgrave Macmillan

2 https://www.haaretz.com/israel-news/business/dov-seidman-s-secret-you-don-t-have-to-be-a-sucker-to-succeed–1.447992

Appendix 4

1 Anne Galletta (2013) *Mastering the Semi-Structured Interview and Beyond: From Research Design to Analysis and Publication*, New York University Press, New York.

2 Boyatzis R.E. (1989) *Thematic Analysis and Code Development – Transforming Qualitative Information*, SAGE Publications, California.

3 Gibbs G.R. (2007) *Analyzing Qualitative Data*, SAGE Publications, London.

4 Saldana J. (2009). *The coding manual for qualitative researchers*, SAGE Publications, California

5 Greg S. Guest and Kathleen M. MacQueen (2012) *Applied Thematic Analysis*, SAGE Publications, California

6 Hlupic V. (2014) *The Management Shift – How to Harness the Power of People and Transform Your Organisation for Sustainable Success*, Palgrave Macmillan

The Humane Capital® Board Game

The Humane Capital® board game delivers an alternative, practical approach that any employer can implement in order to overcome the unique challenges faced by their organization. It explores the steps that businesses need to take in order to become a 'good' organization, doing well by doing good, that can achieve long-term results, and is highly complementary to the book. Through gamification, the Humane Capital® vision and methodology can be shared and cascaded easily and effectively to a diverse audience.

The game demonstrates how current leaders and managers can start the process of shifting their own organisations from 'controlled and orderly' to 'enthusiastic and collaborative'. It begins by providing a vocabulary and structure for the senior team to explore the 8 Pillars of Humane Capital®. Next, it considers the sector specific strategies the organisation could utilise to work on the Pillar themes, creates the awareness of the potential 'barriers' it might encounter on the way, finally focusing on one specific strategy to implement first.

The game :
- Provides a safe environment for experiential learning
- Introduces the vocabulary, structure and philosophy of the Humane Capital® approach to the senior team
- Enables the Humane Capital® vision to be shared and cascaded with the wider organisation
- Provides insight into the 8 Pillars and the impact on the organisation and HOW to practically start to address these
- Facilitates a clearer understanding of the impact of mindset and motivation on the organisation
- Helps the team recognise the potential 'barriers to shifting', enabling the team to identify clear sector specific strategies to start the 'shift'

The game provides any senior team and executive education providers with an easy and accessible step to envision, articulate and begin the process of enabling their organisation to become more humane, high performing and productive.

Further information is available at http://www.themanagementshift.com/humane-capital-book-2

INDEX